D1736513

In celebration of your retirement! Go out and have fun and enjoy your life. Best wishes, from your friend, Karen

SALADE II

PASCALE BEALE

SALADE II

More Recipes from the Market Table

Foreword by

TRACEY RYDER

m27

PUBLISHED BY

M27 Editions LLC, Santa Barbara, California

SALADE II: More Recipes from the Market Table
by Pascale Beale

Copyright 2020 by Pascale Beale and M27 Editions
Foreword Copyright by Tracey Ryder

All rights reserved. No part of this book may be reproduced or
transmitted in any form or by any means electronic or mechanical,
including photocopying, recording, or by any information storage
and retrieval system, without written permission from the publisher.

Second Printing

ISBN 978-0-99-686356-8
Library of Congress Catalog 2019950446

Design and Production by Media 27

M27EDITIONS.COM

Printed in China

For Sasha

Contents

Foreword

SALAD IS A SERIOUS TOPIC. It is also a wildly creative and exciting one. With most eaters today heeding advice to incorporate more fresh, unprocessed, plant-based foods into their diets, the choices are endless, and at times, can seem overwhelming. Even Michael Pollan famously proclaimed in his book, *In Defense of Food: An Eater's Manifesto,* that we should all "Eat food. Not too much. Mostly plants." The reinforcement of this message is everywhere today.

Thankfully, Pascale Beale is a tireless champion of fresh ingredients, and thus, of dazzlingly fresh, absolutely inspired recipes that turn the task of incorporating salads into your daily routine into an enormous culinary gift. With 40 new recipes included in *Salade II*, this is the perfect opportunity to re-think your entire approach to salads. Rather than celebrating fresh ingredients throughout four seasons of the year, it is as if each day has its own season — what is at the pinnacle of ripeness today will be a little less so tomorrow, yet something new will then be at its peak. And in true Pascale fashion, every recipe found on these pages is imbued with a pure sense of abundance. From the bright earthiness of the Artichoke,

Chanterelle and Spring Greens Salad to the savory richness of Black Lentils with Roasted Eggplant and Tomatoes, every bite is revelatory.

I once had the pleasure of teaching a recipe writing class with Pascale Beale. We had known each other for many years at that time and had socialized and shared meals around the same table, but what struck me that day was how utterly beautiful her techniques were. I still vividly recall how effortlessly she inserted a fork into a half of lemon and then twisted it to extract its juice and the way she laid salad greens on top of the utensils to save them from absorbing too much dressing before it was time to toss and serve the salad. Everything she did that day was impressive, and so absolutely simple and elegant. It is often said that the best way to teach is to show, not tell. Pascale certainly accomplished that, and for the first time, I learned how to approach the act of creating from her perspective. This book, to all of our great pleasure, is about showing you how to prepare the finest salads you can imagine.

Tracey Ryder is cofounder of Edible Communities — a network of nearly 80 regional food magazines — and winner of the James Beard Publication of the Year Award.

Cheers and good eating,
Tracey Ryder

Introduction

ALEXIS SOYER, the renowned 19th century French chef once wrote, "What is more refreshing than salads when your appetite seems to have deserted you, or even after a capacious dinner — the nice, fresh, green, and crisp salad, full of life and health, which seems to invigorate the palate." I could not agree more. As I wrote in the introduction to the original *Salade*, "There are few foods that I would happily eat every day of the year. I enjoy the ease with which they can be put together, the endless variations — from light mixed greens to more substantial salad-as-a-meal types — and the fact that I always feel so good when I eat them." This new, revised edition of *Salade* is a continued celebration of my favorite dish.

It has been five years since that first edition of *Salade* was published. Earlier this year, my publisher called me to let me know that the fourth printing of the book was nearly sold out! "We have a decision to make" he said. "Either go back on press with a fifth printing, or this would be the time to update the book, and create *Salade Deux*." The decision was easy, "Let's do a revised edition," I replied, particularly as I had already created a multitude of new salad recipes.

The new salads came about because of the Eat Local Challenge, an annual event sponsored by *Edible* Santa Barbara, the magazine I am a columnist for. The Challenge encourages people to take a personal pledge to only eat and drink locally produced products for an entire month, and every October for the past eight years I have endeavored to do so.

Last year, I decided to add a personal challenge: to create a new salad recipe every day. I documented my progress by posting images of each dish on my Instagram feed. On day thirteen, a friend posted a comment, "Super creative, keep it up! I want to see more." To which I replied, "Thank you Yumi, I love doing this, who knows, maybe it will lead to *Salade Deux!*" It did. Of the forty new salads in this book, fifteen came from that month-long exercise. I enjoyed creating the new dishes so much I kept going. What was originally planned as twenty new dishes, morphed into forty. The book you hold in your hands now, combines the classics from *Salade* with recipes inspired, as before, by my visits to my local farmers' markets.

The marvelous result of the Eat Local Challenge is that by only using locally sourced produce, you eat produce at its freshest and most flavorful. Not long ago, everyone ate locally sourced foods as this was all that was available. Now, with the advent of refrigeration, different growing techniques and mass transportation systems, many foods are available in most parts of the world year-round. That doesn't mean, however, that they taste good. Anyone who has tasted a bland, mealy tomato, grown under heat lamps in the dead of winter can attest to that, particularly when compared to freshly picked off the vine, juicy, sun-ripened tomatoes. There

is no comparison. I was fortunate to learn about seasonality as a young child, when I would accompany my grandmother on her daily rounds, shopping for produce. She would examine every single item to assess its ripeness and taught me to do the same. Although she had never heard of Julia Child, they were quite similar in their approach to cooking. She shared Julia's adage, "You don't have to cook fancy or complicated masterpieces — just good food from fresh ingredients." The manner in which she chose and then prepared even the simplest salad was a testament to that maxim. She was the first person who taught me the art of making salads (see page 20) and I have tried to live up to her expectations ever since.

Years later, when visiting my grandparents' home as an adult, I would cook for them. They initially thought that my "salade composé" or mixed salads filled with unusual ingredients (fruit and nuts for example) were rather odd, and perhaps inspired by some modern newfangled trend. Yet these types of salads are, in fact, centuries old. Written 2000 years ago, Columella's epic work *De Re Rustica*, describes a salad of fresh mint, cilantro, leeks and parsley, thyme, fresh cheese dressed with olive oil, vinegar, salt and pepper. What could be more moderne? I won them over in the end.

I would have liked to show my grandmother John Evelyn's cookbook dedicated solely to salads — *Acetaria: A Discourse on Sallets*, published in 1699 in which he wrote, "We have said how necessary it is that in the composure of a sallet, every plant should come in to bear its part, without being overpower'd by some herb of a stronger taste so as to endanger the native sapor and virtue of the rest; but fall into their places, like the notes in music, in which there should be nothing harsh or grating: And though admitting some discords (to distinguish and illustrate the rest) striking in all the more sprightly, and sometimes gentler

notes, reconcile all dissonances, and melt them into an agreeable composition." She would have appreciated his particular attention to using only the freshest ingredients, and in creating harmony with them.

From Columella's work, through recipes preserved in centuries of cookbooks, written across all continents, one common thread stands out: cook with the freshest local ingredients. For the past year, I have truly savored the extraordinary produce, so painstakingly grown by the farmers in this region. They have nourished my soul and inspiration. The result of all that good food is the compendium of recipes in *Salade II*.

The prominent horticultural scientist, George Ellwanger, wrote a book in 1902 entitled *The Pleasures of the Table*. In the opening lines of the chapter on salads, he wrote, "To remember a successful salad is generally to remember a successful dinner; at all events, the perfect dinner necessarily includes the perfect salad." I hope the salads in this book lead to many successful dinners.

Bon Appetit!

Salad Basics

This is the method I use for making almost all of the salads in this book. It is quick and simple, and you only need one bowl. This basic recipe will make enough vinaigrette for a salad for 6-8 people.

Ingredients

3 tablespoons extra virgin olive oil (use first cold pressed if possible)

1 tablespoon vinegar

Pinch of sea salt

Freshly ground black pepper

1

Pour the olive oil and vinegar into a large salad bowl. Add the salt and 2–3 grinds of black pepper into the bowl. Whisk together to form an emulsion.

2

Place salad utensils over the vinaigrette.

3

Place the salad greens on top of the utensils, ensuring that they do not fall into the vinaigrette. They will wilt if left in the vinaigrette for too long. Leave the salad in the bowl, without tossing it, until you are ready to serve.

4

When ready to serve the salad, use the utensils and toss the greens well.

Vinaigrettes

Simple Vinaigrette

3 tablespoons olive oil

1 tablespoon red wine vinegar

Pinch of sea salt

4–5 grinds of black pepper

Combine all the ingredients in a small bowl and whisk together vigorously to form an emulsion.

Refrigerated, this vinaigrette will keep for 2 weeks. If it separates, re-whisk it to recreate the emulsion. This vinaigrette can be used on all green salads. Use a lighter vinegar (white wine or perhaps an apple cider) when serving with delicate greens, such as mache (lamb's lettuce) or butter lettuce. Use a more robust vinegar, such as Jerez or balsamic when serving heartier greens, such as mesclun, dandelion, arugula or spinach.

Lemon Vinaigrette

3 tablespoons olive oil

Zest and juice of 1 lemon

1 teaspoon white wine vinegar

Pinch of sea salt

2–3 grinds of white pepper

Whisk all of the ingredients together to create a smooth emulsion.

Refrigerated, this vinaigrette will keep for 3–4 days. Shake well before using. This vinaigrette is delicious served with chicken salads, and salads with fennel, apples, celery and endives.

Mustard Vinaigrette

1 tablespoon Dijon mustard

¼ cup olive oil

1 tablespoon red wine vinegar or fig balsamic vinegar

Pinch of sea salt and black pepper

Combine the mustard, olive oil and vinegar in the bottom of a large salad bowl and whisk together to form a thick emulsion. Add a little salt and pepper, and whisk again.

This vinaigrette has the consistency of a light mayonnaise. It is excellent with potato or egg salads, tuna salads or mixed green salads.

Tomato Vinaigrette

¼ cup olive oil

Zest and juice of 1 lemon

1 large red tomato or 6–7 cherry tomatoes — chopped

Pinch of sea salt

Black pepper

Purée all the ingredients in a food processor or blend using an immersion blender in a tall cylinder until you have a smooth vinaigrette. It will have the consistency of a light mayonnaise.

This vinaigrette is fresh and fruity. It is delicious with most green salads and salads that have feta or goat cheese in them. Refrigerated, it will keep for 2–3 days.

Pesto Vinaigrette

¼ cup olive oil

½ bunch cilantro — chopped

½ bunch basil — chopped

1 tablespoon chives — chopped

Juice and zest of 1 lemon

Juice and zest of 1 lime

Pinch of sea salt

Black pepper

Place all of the ingredients in a blender or food processor. Purée until you have a smooth pesto.

This is a zesty vinaigrette that works well with potatoes, pasta, over asparagus and with roasted vegetables. You can store this in the fridge for 3–4 days.

Juice Vinaigrette

⅓ cup carrot juice

⅓ cup orange juice

⅓ cup golden beet juice

⅓ cup olive oil

1 tablespoon white wine vinegar

Pinch of sea salt

Black pepper

Combine all the ingredients in a bowl and whisk together well. This is a fairly thin vinaigrette so a little goes a long way.

If you don't use it immediately, you might have to whisk it again as it may separate a little. Refrigerated, this will keep for 2–3 days. It's wonderful with carrot salads, vegetable salads and with kale and spinach salads.

These vinaigrettes are used throughout the book with slight variations depending on the salad. There are others (avocado, blue cheese and yogurt, for example) that I use for specific salads. These are listed in the index under vinaigrettes.

GREEN SALADS

Petite Salade Verte

~

Salade Verte aux Herbes

~

Spinach, Baby Gem and
Pomegranate Salad

~

Winter Greens Salad with
Goat Cheese and Herbs

~

Grilled Baby Gem and
Pepitas Pesto Salad

~

Romanesco Broccoli,
Purple Cauliflower and
Arugula Salad

~

Carol's Herb and
Nasturtium Salad

~

Arugula Salad with
Shaved Pecorino and
Caramelized Onions

~

Microgreen and
Marigold Salad

~

Artichoke, Chanterelle and
Spring Greens Salad

~

Herb Salad with Late
Summer Peaches, Goat
Cheese and Blistered
Almonds

~

Kale and Spinach Salad
with Honeyed Shallots
and Plums

Petite Salade Verte

It all began with this salad. This is the salad my grandmother made every day. It's the salad we ate at home, and it's the first salad I learnt how to make. She would painstakingly rinse the greens, dry the leaves delicately in a tea towel and assemble it just a couple of minutes before dinner. Sometimes she'd add chives, which she would cut with scissors hanging from a hook underneath her kitchen cabinets, kept specifically for that purpose. It was so simple and refreshing.

The key is getting absolutely fresh salad greens. Mix your greens or use only one type — it all works. I like adding butter lettuce to this simple salad. The leaves are crisp yet soft, their texture a nice counterpoint to other greens.

Serves 8 people

1 shallot — peeled and very finely diced

2 teaspoons Dijon mustard

3 tablespoons olive oil

1 tablespoon cider vinegar or other light vinegar of your choice

Sea salt and black pepper

12 oz mixed salad greens

1 Place the diced shallot with a pinch of salt in a small bowl and stir to combine. Set aside for 5 minutes.

2 Place the mustard in a large salad bowl. Slowly drizzle in the olive oil and vinegar, and whisk until the vinaigrette resembles the consistency of a light mayonnaise. Add salt and pepper to taste. Toss in the diced shallot and stir to combine. Place salad servers over the vinaigrette.

3 Add the mixed greens to the salad bowl, on top of the servers. When you are ready to serve the salad, toss the salad so that all the ingredients are well combined.

Salade Verte aux Herbes

Imagine walking through a herb garden and picking a few leaves from each of the plants as you stroll past them. If you cup your hands around the leaves, the aroma of the herbs — their oils perfuming the tips of your fingers — will be enchanting. The more herbs the better. The wonderful thing about this salad is that it's slightly different each time. If you don't grow your own herbs — no problem — try the selection listed below. If you have more of one than another, that's okay too. Do watch out for herbs that have a very strong aroma such as tarragon (a little goes a long way) or rosemary, which I would not recommend.

Serves 8 people

1/4 cup olive oil

1 tablespoon aged red wine vinegar or sherry vinegar

Zest of 1 lemon

Sea salt and black pepper to taste

12 oz mixed field greens — preferably with arugula in the mix

1 tablespoon dill — finely chopped

1 tablespoon fresh, small basil leaves — left whole

1 tablespoon fresh chives — finely chopped

1 tablespoon fresh Italian parsley — finely chopped

1 tablespoon fresh cilantro — stems removed, leaves left whole

1 Pour the olive oil and vinegar into a large salad bowl and whisk until the vinaigrette is homogeneous. Add the lemon zest, salt and pepper. Whisk again.

2 Place the serving utensils in the bowl over the vinaigrette. Place all the chopped herbs and the mixed greens on top of the utensils. Do not let any of the greens sit in the vinaigrette. The greens will wilt if they sit in the vinaigrette for any length of time. When you are ready to serve the salad, remove the serving utensils and toss the salad.

Note: People's taste in vinaigrettes vary considerably. This recipe can be made more or less strong by adding more or less vinegar. If too much olive oil is added, the vinaigrette will separate.

Spinach, Baby Gem and Pomegranate Salad

Finding tantalizingly shiny, naturally-polished red pomegranates at the farmers' market is a telltale sign that autumn has arrived. The fruit, when split open, reveal their glistening contents; juicy, jewel-like seeds that lend a sweet pop to any dish.

As I like the marriage of sweet, salty and savory flavors in salads, I decided to feature pomegranates and raw peanuts during a cooking demonstration I gave last autumn in a sun-filled olive oil store called Viva Oliva in Montecito, California. As luck would have it, they had a pomegranate balsamic vinegar, whose sweet, yet tart notes mirrored the qualities of the fruit and the nuts. I used the vinegar to make a complementary vinaigrette. I liked the combination so much that I used it for this salad. The honeyed flavor of the emulsion balances the fruity, herbaceous, and earthy crunch of the salad.

Serves 8 people

For the salad:

1/2 lb baby spinach leaves

2–3 heads baby gem lettuce — any wilted exterior leaves removed, then leaves separated and cleaned

1/2 cup packed basil leaves

Seeds from 1 pomegranate

4 oz raw peanuts

6 sprigs dill — thick stems removed

For the vinaigrette:

1/4 cup olive oil

1 tablespoon pomegranate balsamic vinegar (or regular balsamic)

1/2 tablespoon Champagne vinegar

Large pinch of coarse sea salt

7–8 grinds of black pepper

1 On a large platter, arrange the spinach, baby gem and basil leaves in an attractive manner, interspersing the different leaves and colors.

2 Alternate tablespoonfuls of the pomegranate seeds and raw peanuts in a meandering S pattern across the center of the leaves. Tuck the small dill sprigs into the pomegranate seeds.

3 In a small bowl, whisk together the vinaigrette ingredients to form an emulsion. When ready to serve, pour the vinaigrette over the salad.

Winter Greens Salad with Goat Cheese and Herbs

Winter food is so often full of soups and stews (which I adore by the way), but it's nice to freshen things up a bit with a salad like this one. It's a simple winter green salad to brighten up even the wettest and coldest of days.

Serves 8 people

1 tablespoon mustard

¼ cup olive oil

1 tablespoon red wine vinegar or fig balsamic vinegar

Sea salt and black pepper

12 oz mixed winter greens (if you can find pea greens add them to the mix too, and perhaps some watercress)

4–6 oz fresh, crumbled goat cheese

2 tablespoons parsley — finely chopped

2 tablespoons cilantro — finely chopped

1 tablespoon chives — finely chopped

1 Combine the mustard, olive oil and vinegar in the bottom of a large salad bowl and whisk together to form a thick emulsion. Add a little salt and pepper and whisk again. Place serving utensils over the vinaigrette and then place all the salad greens, herbs and goat cheese on top of the utensils.

2 When you are ready to serve the salad, toss it gently so that everything is well combined.

Grilled Baby Gem and Pepitas Pesto Salad

I bake bread almost every week. It literally satisfies my soul, to say nothing of the delectable aroma that fills the house as the bread is baking. I also like to experiment with new fillings and flavors. Recently, I have been on something of a raw pumpkin seed binge, adding them to everything from the sourdough boules to toppings for roasted vegetables. I mentioned this to Norma, the lady I buy them from on a weekly basis at my local farmers' market. She described a pesto she made with the pepitas. It sounded so tempting that I bought more seeds and went home to experiment. The first batch of pesto I blended, I slathered on toasted sourdough topped with sliced heirloom tomatoes. With the second, I made this salad. It has become a family favorite. Thank you, Norma, for the inspiration!

Serves 8 people

For the pesto:

1 cup cilantro leaves

1 cup basil leaves

1 cup raw pepitas
    (raw pumpkin seeds)

½ cup olive oil

Zest and juice of 1 lemon

2 large pinches of coarse
    sea salt

8-10 grinds of black pepper

1 oz grated Parmesan

1 green tomato —
    roughly chopped

For the salad:

4 heads baby gem lettuce —
    any wilted exterior leaves
    removed, then quartered
    lengthwise

Olive oil

4 green tomatoes —
    cut into eighths

Salt

Black pepper

1 In a food processor fitted with a metal blade, chop the cilantro, basil and pepitas using short pulses until the mixture resembles a coarse paste. Add the remaining pesto ingredients, and process until the pesto is fairly smooth.

2 Heat a grill pan over medium-high heat.

3 Place the baby gem quarters into a medium mixing bowl and drizzle with a little olive oil. Toss to coat. Grill the baby gems for just 1-2 minutes per side. They cook quickly — be careful not to char them. Place the grilled lettuce, and the chopped tomatoes onto a serving platter. Sprinkle with a few pinches of salt and 5-6 grinds of pepper.

4 Spoon the pesto over the salad. Serve warm.

Romanesco Broccoli, Purple Cauliflower and Arugula Salad

The only cauliflower I knew growing up was creamy colored with cloud-like florets. Finding multi-hued varieties, such as the lavender-tinted heads featured in this salad, and the magnificently sculptural, chartreuse-colored Romanesco broccoli (also known as Roman cauliflower) has been a visual and gustatory treat. The latter has a crunchier texture, and more delicate, slightly nutty flavor than its pale cousin, which pairs well with the pine nuts in the salad.

Serves 8 people as an accompaniment

For the salad:

Olive oil

1 small head Romanesco broccoli — broken into very small florets

1 head purple cauliflower — broken into very small florets

Coarse sea salt

Black pepper

4 oz baby arugula leaves

1/3 cup pine nuts

For the vinaigrette:

1/3 cup plain yogurt

1/4 cup olive oil

Zest and juice of 1 large lemon

Pinch of salt

4–5 grinds of black pepper

1 Pour 2 tablespoons olive oil into a large skillet placed over medium heat. Once hot, add the broccoli and cauliflower florets to the pan. Sprinkle with a good pinch of salt and 8–10 grinds of pepper. Sauté for 5–6 minutes, stirring frequently. The florets should be just slightly golden and still a little crunchy in texture. You may have to cook the florets in batches depending on the size of your skillet. Add a little more olive oil to the pan if you have to do a second batch.

2 Place the cooked florets onto a large shallow platter or into a salad bowl. Let cool for 5 minutes. Combine with the arugula leaves.

3 Place the pine nuts in a small skillet over medium heat. Dry roast them until they are just golden brown and releasing their aroma, only 1–2 minutes. Scatter the pine nuts over the salad.

4 In a small bowl, whisk the vinaigrette ingredients together to form an emulsion. Pour the vinaigrette over the salad and toss to combine.

Carol's Herb and Nasturtium Salad

Not long ago, my good friend Carol called and asked if I would make a salad for a bridal shower she was giving. She requested a peach salad, and brought over the platter on which it was to be served. The result was this very colorful, vibrant and fresh mélange.

You can also vary the fruit, with a mixture of nectarines, pluots and white peaches, and use different flowers, creating a new edible palette each time.

Serves 8 people

For the salad:

8 oz assorted salad greens

1/4 cup packed basil leaves

1/4 cup packed mint leaves

1/4 cup packed cilantro leaves

4 large yellow peaches — halved, pitted and sliced

2 tablespoons finely chopped chives

12 nasturtium flowers

1/4 cup raw peanuts

For the vinaigrette:

3 tablespoons olive oil

Zest and juice of 1 lemon

2 teaspoons white wine vinegar or Champagne vinegar

Pinch of salt

4–5 grinds of black pepper

1 Cover a large platter with the salad greens, basil, mint and cilantro leaves. Tuck the peach slices into the greens. Scatter the chives, flowers and raw peanuts over the salad.

2 In a small bowl, whisk together all the vinaigrette ingredients to form an emulsion. When ready to serve the salad, pour the vinaigrette over the greens.

Arugula Salad with Shaved Pecorino and Caramelized Onions

I absolutely love caramelized onions. Maybe that's why a Tarte a l'Onion is one of my favorite dishes. This salad is akin to an onion tart without the tart shell. The onions cook slowly, become golden brown, soft and sweet. The shaved Pecorino (you can use other hard cheeses such as Manchego or Parmesan) adds a salty-nutty element that plays well with the pepperiness of the arugula. Try to serve it whilst the onions are still warm — it's even better that way!

Serves 8 people

Olive oil (for cooking the onions)

2–3 large yellow onions — peeled, halved and thinly sliced

1 teaspoon honey

1 teaspoon fresh thyme leaves

Coarse sea salt and pepper

1/3 cup olive oil

2 tablespoons fig balsamic vinegar

8 oz fresh arugula

1/2 bunch cilantro — finely chopped

4 oz Pecorino — use a cheese slicer to make thin shavings

1 Pour a little olive oil into a medium-sized skillet placed over medium-high heat. Add the sliced onions, honey and thyme leaves. Cook, stirring frequently, for 8–10 minutes. Reduce the heat, add some coarse sea salt and pepper and let the onions soften until golden brown. Set aside.

2 Pour the olive oil and vinegar into the bottom of a large salad bowl and whisk together. Place salad utensils over the vinaigrette and place the arugula and cilantro over the utensils. When you are ready to serve the salad, toss it gently so that the ingredients are well combined.

3 Divide the salad equally between eight plates. Spoon an equal amount of the caramelized onions on top of the arugula and cilantro mixture. Place some of the shaved Pecorino on top of the onions.

Microgreen and Marigold Salad

Norma Ortiz is a microgreen-growing powerhouse. She grows an abundant, vibrant, colorful array of nutritious sprouts, nuts, beans, legumes and microgreens in Ojai, California. I discovered her flavorful treats at the Santa Barbara Farmers Market, and have been a devoted fan of her produce ever since.

Drawn to the startling color of amaranth, I started making salads with different microgreens grouped together across large serving platters. Call it painting with sprouts, if you will. Part of the charm of the salad is that, depending on the microgreens and sprouts available at any given time of year, the colorful combinations you can create will vary with the seasons.

Serves 8 people

For the salad:

1 oz onion microgreens

2 oz radish microgreens

2 oz amaranth microgreens

1 oz rambo radish microgreens

12 small assorted cherry tomatoes — quartered

4 marigold blossoms

1 red carrot

For the vinaigrette:

3 tablespoons olive oil

1 tablespoon fig balsamic vinegar

Pinch of salt

1 Across the middle of a large platter, arrange the green-colored onion and radish microgreens into three large mounds, leaving a 1-inch gap between them. Lace the violet-colored amaranth microgreens around and between them. Place the purple rambo microgreens in two bunches diagonally across from each other.

2 Dot the salad with the cut tomatoes and the marigolds.

3 Peel the carrot completely into long thin strips. Roll up the strips and stand them upright, tucked into the microgreens.

4 In a small bowl, vigorously whisk together the olive oil, vinegar and salt to form an emulsion. When ready to serve, spoon the vinaigrette over the microgreens and on top of the tomatoes. The vinaigrette will quickly wilt the microgreens, so only dress this salad just before serving.

Artichoke, Chanterelle and Spring Greens Salad

The inspiration for this salad came together as I gathered ingredients in my basket, walking through a local, springtime farmers' market. For the first time in years, thanks to drought-ending rains, there was an abundance of fresh chanterelles. I was almost giddy with delight when I saw them. What a treat! On the same day, I also found baby purple artichokes and snap peas from one of my favorite local farmers, Jacob Grant, whose spectacular produce is featured in salads throughout this book. As soon as I returned home, I made this salad for lunch. Any salad with sautéed mushrooms in it is a favorite of mine. This one is no exception.

Serves 8 people

For the salad:

4 heads assorted baby gem lettuce — any wilted exterior leaves removed, then leaves separated and cleaned

½ lb snap peas — ends trimmed, then cut on a bias lengthways

3 oz assorted sprouts or microgreens (I used a mix of alfalfa, broccoli, radish, and onion)

½ lb asparagus — spears thinly cut on a bias

6–8 small purple artichokes

Juice of 1 lemon

1 tablespoon butter

Olive oil

½ lb chanterelle mushrooms — cleaned and sliced

Sea salt

Black pepper

¼ lb raw peanuts

For the vinaigrette:

¼ cup olive oil

1 tablespoon Dijon mustard

Zest and juice of 1 lemon

1 tablespoon white wine vinegar or Champagne vinegar

Large pinch of sea salt

8–10 grinds of black pepper

1 On a large platter or shallow serving bowl, arrange the baby gem leaves, snap peas, assorted sprouts and sliced asparagus in an attractive manner, interspersing the different leaves and colors.

2 Trim the stem end of each artichoke and remove any rough outer leaves. Cut in half lengthwise and place in a bowl of water with the lemon juice.

3 Cook the artichokes in a vegetable steamer until just barely tender, about 5–6 minutes. Remove them from the steamer and pat dry.

4 While the artichokes are steaming, melt the butter with 1 tablespoon of olive oil in a large skillet placed over medium heat. Add the chanterelles, a good pinch of sea salt and 6–7 grinds of pepper, and cook until golden brown, about 4–5 minutes. Scatter the cooked chanterelles, and the raw peanuts over the salad.

5 Pour 2 tablespoons olive oil into the same skillet, placed over medium heat. Add the steamed artichoke halves, cut-side down, to the pan and cook for 3–4 minutes. Turn the artichokes cut-side up, season with a little salt and pepper, and cook for 1–2 minutes, before turning them once more to finish the cooking, cut-side down, for another 1–2 minutes. They should have a nice golden color.

6 Arrange the cooked artichokes cut-side up on top of the salad.

7 In a small bowl, whisk the vinaigrette ingredients together to form an emulsion. Pour the vinaigrette over the salad and serve.

Herb Salad with Late Summer Peaches, Goat Cheese and Blistered Almonds

For many years the city of Santa Barbara, California was home to the SOL (sustainable, organic, local) Food Festival. Imagine a park filled with thousands of SOL food enthusiasts, meandering past turkeys, chickens in very stylish coops, and displays of everything from organic gardening to organic wines. Many attendees participated in workshops or watched demonstrations on the cooking stage. It was the brainchild of four dedicated people who passionately believed that food should be grown naturally. I was thrilled to participate in the event, usually doing demonstrations and being a judge in their iron chef-styled competition. One year, I taught a hands-on class showcasing produce from local farms. This was the salad I created for that event. Sadly, the festival no longer takes place, however, its founders are still very much involved with all things SOL, and have inspired me to do the same.

Serves 8 people

For the vinaigrette:

4 tablespoons olive oil

Juice of 2 lemons

10 cherry tomatoes

Pinch of sea salt

4–5 grinds of black pepper

For the salad:

6 oz mixed salad greens with lots of herbs — try to include some purple basil and dill if possible

1 tablespoon finely chopped chives

6–8 peaches — cut into thin slices (if they are large, 4 will suffice)

8 oz goat cheese — cut into thin slices

4 oz salted almonds

1   Whisk together the olive oil and lemon juice in a salad bowl. Using a fork, crush the tomatoes in a small bowl. Add them to the vinaigrette. Add the salt and pepper and stir to combine. Place salad utensils on top of the vinaigrette.

2   Place all of the remaining ingredients in the salad bowl, on top of the salad utensils. When ready to serve, gently toss the salad so that the peach slices and goat cheese slices stay intact.

Kale and Spinach Salad with Honeyed Shallots and Plums

This salad came about during the photo shoot for this book. I had just picked the first plums of the season from my tree. They sat glistening on the counter top. They were juicy and sweet. I thought they would pair nicely with the roasted kale and made a test version of the salad. We liked it so much I never made the original salad planned for that day's photo session. The juice from the plums combines with the vinaigrette, creating a sweet counterpoint to the salty-crunchy texture of the kale and pecans. It's good with a little cheese, too — perhaps some feta, goat or a crumbled blue.

Serves 8 people

2 bunches kale — cleaned, stem ends trimmed and then cut into 1-inch wide strips

Olive oil

Sea salt and black pepper

12 shallots — peeled and quartered

1 tablespoon honey

10–12 plums — cut into eighths

1 tablespoon chives — finely chopped

3/4 cup pecan halves

1 tablespoon Dijon mustard

1/4 cup olive oil

1 tablespoon red wine vinegar

8 oz spinach

1 Preheat oven to 350 degrees.

2 Place the kale on a baking sheet and drizzle lightly with olive oil. Toss to coat. Sprinkle with some salt and pepper. Bake in the center of the oven for 8 minutes.

3 While the kale is roasting, pour a little olive oil into a cast-iron skillet or heavy-bottomed pan placed over medium heat. Add the shallots and cook for 5 minutes, turning occasionally. Add the honey and plums and cook for 5 minutes more. Add the chives and pecans, a little black pepper and toss the ingredients to combine. Remove from the heat.

4 Place the mustard in the bottom of a large salad bowl and whisk in 1/4 cup olive oil and the vinegar to form a smooth emulsion. It should look like a light mayonnaise. Add the shallot-plum mixture, the roasted kale and the spinach. Toss to combine all the ingredients well. Serve while the kale is still warm.

APPLE & PEARS

Green Apple, Herb
and Green Tomato
Salad

—

Apple, Cucumber and
Champagne Grape
Salad

—

Pear, Arugula and
Mint Salad

—

Salad with Glazed
Apples and Goat
Cheese

—

Pear and Fennel
Salad

—

Kale, Apple and
Almond Salad

—

Pear Carpaccio
with a Mache and
Roquefort Salad

—

Apple and Baby Gem
Salad

Green Apple, Herb and Green Tomato Salad

I recently found some irresistible gooseberry-like green tomatoes at the farmers' market. They had almost translucent, iridescent skin that glistened as the sun shone on them. They had a firm texture and nice acidity, which oddly made me think of crunchy green apples. Once back in my kitchen, I made a small salad with the two fruit, and was delighted that they worked so well together.

Paired with the freshness of the mint leaves and perfume from the lemon basil, this salad is crisp, bright and light.

Serves 8 people

For the salad:

4 green crunchy unpeeled apples — very thinly sliced, on a mandolin if possible

1/2 lb green cherry tomatoes — quartered

30 small mint leaves

30 small lemon basil leaves (if you cannot find lemon basil, use regular Italian basil)

1/4 cup lightly toasted pine nuts

For the vinaigrette:

3 tablespoons olive oil

Zest and juice of 1 lemon

1 tablespoon lime juice

Coarse sea salt

Black pepper

1 Completely cover a large platter with the apple slices, overlapping them slightly. Scatter the chopped green tomatoes, mint and basil leaves, and toasted pine nuts over the apples.

2 In a small bowl whisk together the olive oil, lemon zest and juice, and lime juice to form an emulsion. Immediately pour the vinaigrette over the apples to prevent them from discoloring. Sprinkle the salad with a generous pinch of salt and 5–6 grinds of black pepper.

Apple, Cucumber and Champagne Grape Salad

A friend dropped off a large bag of gem-like, pearl-sized grapes. They instantly reminded me of a dish I had prepared in a cooking class a few years ago — chicken with roasted grapes — and thought they would be wonderful prepared the same way, but this time served in a salad. Their sweetness and texture marry well with the crisp apples and cucumber, and the earthy pepperiness of the globe turnips. Don't be put off by the idea of raw turnips, they are a revelation, and work wonders in all types of salads.

Serves 8 people

For the salad:

3 large unpeeled apples — very thinly sliced, on a mandolin if possible

Zest and juice of 2 small lemons

3 Persian cucumbers — very thinly sliced, on a mandolin if possible

3 Japanese globe turnips — very thinly sliced, on a mandolin if possible

For the vinaigrette:

Olive oil

1/2 lb Champagne grapes — separated into small clusters or de-stemmed entirely

Flake salt

Black pepper

1 Cover the center of eight dinner plates with the apple slices. Spoon a little lemon juice over the apples to prevent them from discoloring.

2 Arrange the sliced cucumbers and turnips on top of the apple slices in an attractive pattern. This does not have to be symmetrical.

3 Pour 1 tablespoon olive oil into a medium-sized skillet placed over medium heat. When the oil is hot, add the grapes and sauté, stirring frequently, for 2–3 minutes. The grapes will just start rendering their juice. Remove from the heat and place the grapes on top of the cucumbers and turnips. Reserve any juice in the pan for the vinaigrette.

4 Sprinkle each salad with some lemon zest.

5 In a small bowl, whisk together the 3 tablespoons olive oil, the remaining lemon juice, plus any grape juice from the pan, to form an emulsion. Spoon the vinaigrette over the plated salads. Sprinkle a little flake salt and 3–4 grinds of black pepper over each one. Serve immediately.

Pear, Arugula and Mint Salad

One very blustery day last winter, I took my lovely dog, Sasha, for a walk on the beach. Nothing pleased her more than running along the sand, chasing waves. The sky that day was spectacular, with great billowing clouds promising rain on the horizon, and giant shards of pale, golden, ethereal light streaming through them, illuminating patches of the wind-torn ocean.

At home, later on, craving a little something to eat after a few hours out in the elements, I sliced open a pear, the color of which immediately made me think of that light, which in turn led me to cutting thinner and thinner slices, which led to this salad. Inspiration for dishes comes from many places—this one from a walk on the beach!

Serves 8 people

For the salad:

8 oz baby arugula

1/2 cup packed mint leaves

1/4 cup packed cilantro leaves

1/2 cup bean sprouts

4 Bosc pears — halved, cored and thinly sliced

2 oz crumbled feta

2 tablespoons finely chopped chives

Flake salt

Black pepper

For the vinaigrette:

1/4 cup olive oil

Juice of 1 Meyer lemon

1 teaspoon white wine vinegar

1 teaspoon finely minced fresh ginger

Pinch of salt

1 Cover the center of a large platter with the arugula, mint, cilantro and bean sprouts.

2 Arrange the pear slices in small fans of 4–6 slices, tucking them into the mixed greens.

3 Scatter the feta and chives over the salad, adding a sprinkling of flake salt and 8–10 grinds of pepper over the top.

4 In a small bowl, whisk together the vinaigrette ingredients to form an emulsion. When ready to serve, pour the vinaigrette over the salad.

Salad with Glazed Apples and Goat Cheese

I love making salads with a warm ingredient in them, particularly when there is cheese. In this case, the warm ingredient is glazed apples. When you toss the salad, the cheese melts a little and mixes with the vinaigrette. It's really scrumptious.

Serves 8 people

4 Granny Smith apples — peeled, cored and thinly sliced

2 tablespoons butter

1 tablespoon light brown sugar

1 tablespoon Dijon mustard

3 tablespoons olive oil

1 tablespoon good, aged red wine vinegar or sherry vinegar

Sea salt and black pepper

6–8 oz mixed field greens — preferably with arugula in the mix

1 tablespoon fresh dill — finely chopped

1 tablespoon fresh basil — finely chopped

1 tablespoon fresh chives — finely chopped

1 tablespoon fresh Italian parsley — finely chopped

5 oz goat cheese

1 Melt the butter in a large skillet placed over medium heat. When the butter foams, toss in the apple slices and sauté until golden brown. Sprinkle the sugar over the apples and cook for a few more minutes until the sugar and butter become syrupy and almost caramelized. Remove the pan from the heat, leaving the apples in the pan until you are ready to assemble the salad.

2 Place one rounded tablespoon of mustard in the bottom of a salad bowl. Slowly drizzle in the olive oil and whisk just until the vinaigrette resembles the consistency of a light mayonnaise. If too much olive oil is added, the vinaigrette will separate. Add the vinegar and whisk until the vinaigrette is homogeneous. Add a pinch of salt and pepper to taste.

3 Place the serving utensils in the bowl over the vinaigrette, then place all the chopped herbs and mixed greens on top of the utensils. Do not let any of the greens sit in the vinaigrette.

4 Crumble the goat cheese into the bowl and add the glazed apples. When you are ready to serve the salad, toss it gently so that everything is well combined.

Pear and Fennel Salad

Pears and fennel are one of those perfect pairings. They complement each other as the anise taste of the crunchy fennel combines with the soft, sweet and slightly grainy pears. Try to find pears that are a little juicy but not overly ripe so that they will hold their shape in the salad. This salad has layers of flavors that mingle with each other in such a way that no two mouthfuls taste exactly alike.

Serves 8 people

4 tablespoons olive oil

3 shallots — peeled, halved and thinly sliced

1 tablespoon aged red wine vinegar or sherry vinegar

Zest of 1 lemon

Sea salt and black pepper

2 oz fresh cilantro — leaves only

1 bunch fresh chives — finely chopped

4 pears — cored, quartered and thinly sliced

2 large fennel bulbs — quartered and thinly sliced

4 oz pistachios or almonds or a mixture of both — roughly chopped

4 oz feta cheese

4 oz fresh arugula

4 oz fresh mixed greens

1 Pour 1 tablespoon of olive oil into a small skillet placed over medium heat. Add the shallots and cook for 5 minutes, stirring frequently. They should be a light golden brown color. Remove the pan from the heat and add the 3 remaining tablespoons of olive oil, the vinegar, lemon zest, a pinch of coarse salt and pepper. Whisk vigorously. Return to the stove for 1–2 minutes.

2 Pour the warm vinaigrette into the bottom of a large salad bowl. Place the serving utensils in the bowl over the vinaigrette. Then place all the chopped herbs, pears, fennel, nuts and feta on top of the utensils. Cover this with the arugula and mixed greens. When you are ready to serve the salad, toss it gently so that everything is well combined.

Kale, Apple and Almond Salad

Kale salads are all the rage right now (well, kale in general). It's become THE hot green, if that's possible. I think that spinach had its glory days some years ago, and then it was arugula's turn. The thing is, I LOVE kale. It's a vegetable I discovered relatively recently. We did not eat kale in London where I grew up. Spinach, yes. Chard, check. Arugula, absolutely. Kale, not a mouthful — until I came to California. Now I add it to everything. It has become another one of my fads, although I think that this one will never fade. I have made tons of kale dishes — roasted kale, crispy kale chips, raw kale salad — well, you get the general idea. Here's one of my favorites.

Serves 8 people

For the vinaigrette:

4 tablespoons olive oil

Juice of 1/2 lemon

2 tablespoons chives — finely chopped

1 tablespoon parsley — finely chopped

1 rounded tablespoon Greek yogurt

Sea salt and black pepper

For the salad:

2 bunches kale — rinsed and chopped

Olive oil

Sea salt and black pepper

Juice of 1 lemon

4–5 apples — cored, quartered and then thinly sliced

1/4 lb almonds — roughly chopped

1 Preheat the oven to 350 degrees.

2 Place all the vinaigrette ingredients in a large salad bowl and whisk together well. Place salad utensils over the vinaigrette.

3 Place the chopped kale on a baking sheet or in a roasting pan. Drizzle with olive oil and toss to coat evenly. Sprinkle with coarse salt and freshly ground black pepper. Roast for 7–8 minutes. The kale will be just wilted and bits of it will be slightly crunchy. As soon as you take the kale out of the oven, pour the lemon juice over it and toss gently.

4 Add the cooked kale and the remaining salad ingredients to the bowl and toss well. This is one salad that actually benefits from being tossed at least 10 minutes before you serve it.

Pear Carpaccio with a Mache and Roquefort Salad

Traditionally, carpaccio is a dish of paper-thin beef or fish that is drizzled with olive oil or lemon juice. In this dish, it's the pears that have been thinly sliced to create the carpaccio. The pears are sliced horizontally to create round disks. You can slice them lengthwise and fan out the pears, if you prefer.

Serves 8 people

3 tablespoons lemon olive oil

1 tablespoon Champagne vinegar

Sea salt and black pepper

4 oz mache

2 oz Roquefort cheese — crumbled

1 bunch chives — finely chopped

1 tablespoon pecans — chopped

1 tablespoon pistachios — chopped

4 Asian pears — peeled and sliced horizontally to create 1/8-inch disks

1 lemon — halved

1   Mix together the olive oil and vinegar in the bottom of a large salad bowl. Add a pinch of salt and some freshly ground black pepper. Place salad utensils over the vinaigrette.

2   Place the mache, Roquefort, chives and nuts on top of the serving utensils and set aside until ready to serve.

3   Arrange the very thinly sliced pear disks in a circular pattern on each salad plate, covering the central part of each plate completely. Squeeze some lemon juice over the pears.

4   Toss the salad and divide it equally between the plates, placing the salad on top of the pears.

Apple and Baby Gem Salad

In an article about baking, I came across a photo of a crisp tart made with closely-packed, thinly-sliced, different-colored apples. The effect was visually striking and mouth-watering. I made the tart and liked it so much I thought I'd try using apples, sliced in the same way, in other dishes. This crunchy, fresh salad is the result.

You can also use different varieties of pears, or mix the two together. Just be sure that their skins are different colors.

Serves 8 people

For the salad:

3 heads assorted baby gem lettuce (or mixed salad greens)

4-5 assorted apples (choose ones with different colored skins) — quartered, cored and thinly sliced

$1/3$ cup packed mint leaves, plus 1 tablespoon finely chopped mint

$1/3$ cup packed basil leaves, plus 1 tablespoon finely sliced basil

$1/4$ lb bean sprouts — chopped

$1/3$ cup chopped salted pistachios

1 tablespoon finely chopped chives

For the vinaigrette:

$1/4$ cup olive oil

Zest and juice of 1 lemon

Zest and juice of 1 lime

Pinch of salt

6-7 grinds of black pepper

1. Cover the center of a large salad bowl with the baby gems (or assorted greens), mint and basil leaves.

2. Arrange the apple slices, by variety, in small fans of 6-7 slices, tucking them into the mixed greens.

3. In a small bowl, thoroughly combine the chopped mint, sliced basil, bean sprouts, pistachios and chives. Spoon this mixture into the center of the salad.

4. In a small bowl, whisk together the vinaigrette ingredients to form an emulsion. Pour the vinaigrette over the salad and serve.

ASPARAGUS

Asparagus, Snap Pea
and Orchid Salad

—

Roasted Purple
Asparagus with
Baby Kale

—

Asparagus Trio
Salad with Arugula
and Basil

—

Asparagus, Salmon
and Herb Verrines

—

White Asparagus
Salad with Olives
and Herb Pesto
Vinaigrette

—

Grilled Asparagus
Salad

Asparagus, Snap Pea and Orchid Salad

Earlier this year, my friend Nicole called to ask me if I would prepare a surprise birthday brunch for her wife, and fellow chef, Cat Cora, which I was delighted to do. Along with avocado toasts with poached eggs, and wild mushroom crostini, I prepared this salad for them, using vibrant edible orchids with the first springtime asparagus and snap peas I had found at the market that weekend. The brunch was a success, and we had a chance to catch up on all things culinary, and chatting about friends and family too. It was a lovely, languorous morning, a treat in our otherwise hectic lives. Hopefully, we'll manage to gather around the table again soon.

This is a lovely celebratory salad, due, in large part, to the color and vibrancy of the orchids. If, however, you cannot find them, don't worry. Other edible flowers, such as nasturtiums, can be just as festive and appetizing.

Serves 8 people

For the vinaigrette:

1/4 cup olive oil

1 tablespoon white wine vinegar or Champagne vinegar

1 tablespoon finely sliced chives

Pinch of salt

4–5 grinds of black pepper

For the salad:

1 lb thick-stemmed asparagus — raw

8 oz assorted mixed greens

8 oz snap peas — ends trimmed and thinly sliced on a bias

1/2 cup basil leaves

3 oz assorted sprouts or microgreens (a mix of alfalfa, broccoli, radish, and onion if possible)

3-inch piece daikon radish — peeled and very thinly sliced

10–12 edible flowers such as dendrobium orchids or nasturtiums

1   In a large salad bowl, vigorously whisk together the vinaigrette ingredients to form an emulsion. Place salad utensils over the vinaigrette.

2   Thinly slice all but 4 of the raw asparagus stalks. Carefully peel the remaining stalks into long thin strips. Tie the strips into loose knots.

3   Place the mixed greens, sliced asparagus, snap peas and basil on top of the salad utensils. Nestle small handfuls of the sprouts throughout the salad. Finish decorating the salad with the sliced daikon, asparagus knots and edible flowers.

4   When ready to serve, toss gently to combine.

Roasted Purple Asparagus with Baby Kale

This salad combines two of my favorite ingredients: asparagus and kale. The purple asparagus adds color and has a slightly more bitter taste than the green variety, which can, of course, be substituted here if you cannot find the purple. This is an easy salad to make and is wonderful on busy weekday evenings, as it takes just minutes to prepare. You can also add all sorts of other ingredients to this. I just made a variation that had green onions, cherry tomatoes and almonds to bring to my book club potluck. These evenings have turned into monthly major vegetarian feasts. A good book to discuss, good friends and good food — what could be better than that?

Serves 8 people

For the salad:

1 large bunch baby kale — chopped

1 bunch mustard greens — chopped

1 bunch pea tendrils — chopped

2 lbs purple asparagus — tips trimmed and the rest of the stalk cut on a bias into 1/2-inch pieces

Olive oil

Sea salt and black pepper

For the vinaigrette:

4 tablespoons olive oil

Juice and zest of 1 lemon

1 tablespoon Champagne vinegar

1 teaspoon fig balsamic vinegar or other fruity balsamic vinegar

40–50 Thai basil leaves

30–40 green basil leaves

1 Preheat the oven to 350 degrees.

2 Place the chopped kale, mustard greens and pea tendrils on a baking sheet or in a shallow roasting pan. Scatter the chopped asparagus over the top of the greens. Drizzle a little olive oil over the vegetables, just to coat. Add a pinch of salt and grind some pepper over the entire dish.

3 Pop the dish into the oven for 7 minutes, turning the vegetables once during the cooking time.

4 While the vegetables are cooking, prepare the vinaigrette. Combine the olive oil with the lemon juice, lemon zest and vinegars in a large salad bowl and whisk together vigorously to make a homogeneous vinaigrette. Add all the greens and the two types of basil and toss well. Serve while the salad is still warm.

Asparagus Trio Salad with Arugula and Basil

This is one of those dishes that was inspired by a walk through the farmers' market. It was in the middle of asparagus season with fresh green stalks piled up everywhere. When I came across some purple asparagus, they were so beautiful to look at, I couldn't resist them. The stalks are a deep burgundy with flashes of green peeking through. The same day, I found some white asparagus in another market. The trio of colors looked so appetizing on my kitchen counter that I decided to make a salad with all three. By a complete coincidence, I had three varieties of basil in my garden and used the small tender leaves from each in the salad. Thai basil is quite strong, so I wouldn't use too much of it, as it may overpower the delicate flavors of the asparagus.

Serves 8 people

Juice and zest of 1 large lemon

5 tablespoons olive oil

Sea salt and black pepper

4 oz arugula

1 small bunch of each green, purple and Thai basil — leaves removed from the stems and left whole

$1/2$ lb each green, white and purple asparagus — tips trimmed and left whole, the rest of the stalk cut on a bias into very thin slices

$1/2$ lb English peas — shelled (that is the shelled weight so you'll need about 2 lbs with the shells on)

1 Pour the lemon juice, 4 tablespoons of olive oil, a pinch of salt and 4–5 grinds of pepper into the bottom of a medium-sized salad bowl. Whisk together well. Place salad utensils over the top of the vinaigrette. Place the arugula and basil leaves on top of the utensils and set aside.

2 Pour the remaining 1 tablespoon of olive oil into a large skillet placed over medium-high heat. Add the sliced asparagus, the asparagus tips, peas and lemon zest and sauté for 3–4 minutes, stirring occasionally. Remove from the heat.

3 Add the asparagus-pea mixture to the salad bowl. Toss all the ingredients until well combined. Divide the salad equally between the plates, The salad is lovely when the asparagus are still warm.

Asparagus, Salmon and Herb Verrines

There is something quite tantalizing about being able to see a dish in its entirety before you delve into it. Usually we look down on our food. The few exceptions are normally reserved for desserts. Ice cream sundaes and other cold desserts come to mind — usually served with one of those long skinny spoons to scoop out all the best bits that have sunk to the bottom. In these verrines, you get the same thing in a savory form.

The inspiration for this dish came from two sources. The first was a book on verrines that I found tucked away on a shelf in my father's house in Provence. I wish I had that book today, for it was chock-full of glass-filled delights. I had the memory of one of the photographs from it when, to my amazement, I came across another version of the smoked salmon and fingerling potatoes salad in Beatrice Peltre's excellent book, *La Tartine Gourmande.* This is my version, made with both salmon filet and smoked salmon, and with some crème fraiche in the yogurt mixture, a touch I know my grandmother from Normandy would have appreciated.

Serves 8 people

1/4 lb small purple potatoes

1/2 lb asparagus — reserving 16 tips for the garnish

1/2 lb haricots verts

2 cups Greek yogurt

2 tablespoons crème fraiche

Zest and juice of 2 lemons

1/2 bunch chives — finely chopped — reserving 1 tablespoon and 16 tips for garnish

2 tablespoons dill — finely chopped

2 tablespoons olive oil

Pinch of sea salt

4–5 grinds of black pepper

8 oz cooked salmon filet or smoked filet of salmon — flaked

8 oz smoked salmon — chopped

1 lemon — quartered

4 oz golden fish roe for garnish

8 sprigs dill (optional)

1. Steam the potatoes until just tender. Let cool and then thinly slice.

2. Steam the asparagus and haricots verts until just al dente. Remove from the steamer and set aside to cool. Both vegetables will need to be trimmed to fit inside the verrines. Slice the haricots verts in half, and the asparagus either in thirds or quarters so that they will fit inside your verrines.

3. Combine the yogurt, crème fraiche, lemon juice and zest, chives, dill and olive oil in a bowl and whisk together well. Add the pepper and a pinch of salt and mix again.

4. Spoon a little of the yogurt mixture into the bottom of each verrine. Lay the haricots verts halves horizontally on top of the yogurt. Divide the salmon filet equally between the verrines, placing it on top of the haricots verts.

5. Spoon a little more of the yogurt mixture over the salmon filet, then top this with the asparagus pieces. Cover the asparagus with remaining yogurt mixture.

6. Arrange the thinly sliced potatoes over the yogurt mixture in each verrine. Layer the smoked salmon over the sliced potatoes.

7. Squeeze a little fresh lemon juice over the salmon just before serving. Garnish with a sprig of dill or chives, the reserved asparagus tips and golden fish roe.

White Asparagus Salad with Olives and Herb Pesto Vinaigrette

I really became enamored of white asparagus on a trip to Austria many years ago. Everywhere we went, white asparagus were on the menu. They were beautiful, fat, juicy asparagus filled with a herbaceous, crisp flavor. Finding white asparagus that are as good as those has become an annual quest. Every now and then I'll come across a really good batch, and this is the salad I make with them.

Serves 8 people

2 lbs. white asparagus — stalks peeled and ends trimmed

3–4 tablespoons black Niçoise olives — pitted and chopped

1 small bunch chives — chopped

Zest of 1 lemon

Zest of 1 lime

Black pepper

For the pesto vinaigrette:

1/4 cup olive oil

1/2 bunch cilantro (about 1 cup) — roughly chopped

1/2 bunch basil — roughly chopped

1 tablespoon parsley — roughly chopped

Juice of 1 lemon

Juice of 1 lime

Large pinch of sea salt

8–10 grinds of black pepper

1   Steam the asparagus for 8–9 minutes. They should be al dente. The white variety takes a little longer to cook than the green, but do take care not to overcook them. As soon as they are cooked, carefully remove the asparagus from the steamer and set aside to cool.

2   While the asparagus are cooking, purée all the pesto ingredients in a blender until smooth. Check the seasoning, adding more lemon juice, if needed. Pour the pesto vinaigrette onto a serving platter so that it covers the bottom of the dish completely.

3   Place the asparagus on top of the vinaigrette and sprinkle them with the chopped olives, chives, and lemon and lime zest. Grind a little black pepper over the top and serve immediately.

Grilled Asparagus Salad

I have one of those cast-iron griddle pans that you can put on top of your stove. I never used it very much until a few years ago when I started to conquer my apprehension about grilling in general. Since I had an aversion to schlepping and cleaning my underused barbecue that lived outside under a tree, I thought I'd give this griddle thing a try. Why did I not do this before? It's fantastic, and so easy to use! Asparagus cooked this way somehow tastes even better. The little charred bits on the stalks are earthy tasting, yet the stalks retain their herbaceous qualities. This is now one of my favorite ways to prepare asparagus.

If you have mastered your barbecue, you can, of course, grill them over hot coals too. Do, however, put them in a vegetable grill basket or pan, otherwise they have the annoying habit of falling through the grill and getting overly singed.

Serves 8 people

For the salad:

1 lb green asparagus — tips left whole, stems cut into 1 1/2-inch pieces

1 lb white asparagus — tips left whole, stems peeled, then cut into 1 1/2-inch pieces

Olive oil

Salt

Black pepper

20-30 small Thai basil leaves

For the vinaigrette:

2 tablespoons olive oil

1 tablespoon lemon juice

1 teaspoon white wine vinegar or Champagne vinegar

1 tablespoon finely chopped dill

1 teaspoon finely chopped chives

1 Place the asparagus in a shallow dish. Lightly drizzle with olive oil, and sprinkle with a generous pinch of salt and 8–10 grinds of black pepper. Shake the dish back and forth a few times to make sure the asparagus spears are coated.

2 Place a cast-iron griddle on the stove over medium-high heat. Once it is hot, lay the asparagus stalks on the griddle and cook for 1 1/2 minutes. Turn once and cook for another minute. The vegetables should still be bright green and al dente. Carefully remove the cooked asparagus and place them on a serving platter, arranged with tips pointing outwards like a giant flower. Dot the salad with basil leaves.

3 In a small bowl, whisk all the vinaigrette ingredients to form an emulsion. Pour over the warm asparagus and serve.

BEETS & RADISHES

Arugula and Radish
Rosettes Salad

—

Golden Beet and
Green Tomato Salad

—

Curry Roasted Golden
Beet Salad

—

Pascale's Birthday
Beet Salad

—

Raw Beet and Goat
Cheese Salad

—

Movers and Shakers
Salad

Arugula and Radish Rosettes Salad

I received this beautiful blue Moroccan bowl as a gift. It appeared on my terrace one morning from my friend Montserrat. Our friendship began with a moving conversation about the first edition of my book *Salade*, and the impact, she told me, that the recipes had on her life. I am always humbled by her gracious and generous comments, and inspired by her vitality and love of life. It was only fitting, therefore, that the first dish I made in this lovely bowl was, of course, a salad. Bon appétit et merci Monserrat!

Serves 8 people

For the salad:

8 oz baby arugula

4–5 long radishes, sometimes known as Japanese radishes, entirely peeled lengthwise to create long thin strips (Japanese radishes can be white or red)

3 medium-sized watermelon radishes — peeled and very thinly sliced, on a mandolin if possible, creating thin petal-like slices

8 Medjool dates — cut into small pieces

1/3 cup pistachios

For the vinaigrette:

1/4 cup basil olive oil

1 1/2 tablespoons aged balsamic vinegar, flavored with pomegranates if possible

Pinch of coarse sea salt

4–5 grinds of black pepper

1 Place the arugula in a medium-sized salad bowl.

2 Roll half the long radish strips to resemble rose buds that are just opening, and nestle them into the arugula. Roll the remaining radish strips in the same fashion, but wrapping them with overlapping slices of larger watermelon radish petals to create two sizes of roses. Nestle each radish rose in the arugula. (Nestling them helps them stay together.)

3 Sprinkle the Medjool date pieces and pistachios over the salad.

4 In a small bowl, whisk together all the vinaigrette ingredients to form an emulsion. Pour the vinaigrette over the salad and serve, taking care to keep the roses whole.

Golden Beet and Green Tomato Salad

Golden beets live up to their name. Sunflower yellow inside, they can transform a dish with a pop of color, and their natural sugars are enhanced when cooked. I couldn't resist the color combination of the golden beets and green tomatoes, hence, this salad.

Serves 8 people

For the salad:

8 medium-sized golden beets — peeled and thinly sliced on a mandolin

Olive oil

1 teaspoon white wine vinegar or pear Champagne vinegar

8 medium-sized green tomatoes — thinly sliced

½ bunch chives — finely chopped

1 bunch basil leaves

Sea salt

For the vinaigrette:

4 tablespoons olive oil

Juice of 1 lemon

Pinch of coarse sea salt

4–5 turns of black pepper

1 Pour a little olive oil into a large skillet placed over medium heat. Place the beet slices in the pan so that they barely overlap (you will probably need to do this in 2 or 3 batches). Drizzle a little of the white wine vinegar over the top, add a pinch of salt and cook for 3–4 minutes, turning the beets once or twice. The beets should be just cooked through. Remove the pan from the heat, leaving the beets in the pan. Cover and let rest for 3–4 minutes.

2 Arrange the beet slices in concentric circles on each plate. Insert a green tomato slice in-between every 3–4 beet slices.

3 Whisk all the vinaigrette ingredients together so that you have a smooth emulsion. Pour the vinaigrette over the beets and tomatoes, then sprinkle with the chopped chives. Insert the basil leaves in-between the beet and tomato slices.

Curry Roasted Golden Beet Salad

I once ate a chicken curry in London that brought tears to my eyes. It was so, so, so spicy, I couldn't eat enough yogurt to squelch the burning sensation in my throat. The person who cooked the curry made his own blend of curry powder (a mixture, which interestingly enough, doesn't really exist in India — curry being a type of food, not an actual spice). He evidently had a heavy hand when it came to hot spices.

Most curry powder recipes include coriander, turmeric, cumin, fenugreek and red pepper, with the possible addition of cardamom, cinnamon, cloves, mustard seeds and ginger. There are huge variations in curry blends. I like to make one that has less heat (I admit that I am a bit of a wimp when it comes to really spicy food). The idea, for me, is to create a dish that has a soupçon of those fragrant flavors but not one that is overpowered by them. This salad is one of those dishes. Beets and curry are delicious together as the spices enrich the sweet earthiness of the beets.

Serves 8 people

For the salad:

Olive oil

4–6 golden beets — cleaned and roots trimmed

Sea salt

6–8 shallots — peeled and quartered

6 oz golden raisins

2 teaspoons of your favorite curry powder

1/2 bunch cilantro leaves — left whole

4 oz feta cheese — crumbled (optional)

For the citrus vinaigrette:

4 tablespoons olive oil

Zest and juice of 1 orange

Zest and juice of 2 lemons

1 teaspoon white wine vinegar

Pinch of sea salt

3–4 grinds of black pepper

1 Preheat the oven to 350 degrees.

2 Place the golden beets on a sheet of foil that is large enough to envelop them. If the beets are very large, you may need to do this in 2 pouches. Drizzle a little olive oil over the beets and sprinkle with some coarse salt. Wrap them completely in the foil. Place the foil pouch(es) on a baking sheet and cook for 30 minutes. The beets should be relatively easy to pierce, but not too soft.

3 While the beets are roasting, prepare the remaining salad ingredients. Pour the vinaigrette ingredients into the bottom of a salad bowl and whisk together well. Place the salad utensils on top of the vinaigrette.

4 Pour a little olive oil into a medium-sized skillet placed over medium heat. Add the shallots, golden raisins and curry powder. Cook for 8–10 minutes or until the shallots are soft and golden. Place the raisin and shallot mixture and the cilantro leaves in the salad bowl.

5 Once the beets are cooked, remove from the oven and foil. Let rest for 10 minutes or until cool enough to handle. Peel the beets and cut them into thin wedges or slices and then add them to the salad bowl.

6 Toss all the ingredients together and let rest 10 minutes before serving. Serve while the beets are still warm. You can also add feta cheese to this salad, which melts a little with the warm beets.

Pascale's Birthday Beet Salad

Last year I celebrated my birthday by having a huge picnic in the middle of a vineyard. It was one of those perfect, sunny, warm spring days. We set up long trestle tables under large oak trees surrounded by acres of vines as far as the eye could see. The tables were laden with salads, cheese, fresh bread, salmon and fruit. This was one of the salads I made that morning. I had originally planned to make a straight beet salad. However, when I realized how many people we were going to be, I kept adding ingredients, and this is the salad it turned into.

Serves 8 to 10 people

6 golden beets

Olive oil

Coarse sea salt

2 long leeks — roots trimmed away, halved and thinly sliced

1 large yellow onion — peeled, halved and thinly sliced

6-8 shallots — peeled and sliced

3 tablespoons golden raisins

1 bunch green onions — root ends trimmed away and then finely chopped

Sea salt and black pepper

1 lb snap peas — trimmed and thinly sliced on a bias

1 lb English peas (1 lb shelled, so you will need at least twice that weight to net 1 lb)

8 oz baby spinach

1 bunch chives — finely chopped

Juice of 2-3 lemons

1 Preheat the oven to 350 degrees.

2 Place the golden beets on a sheet of foil that is large enough to envelop them. If the beets are very large you may need to do this in 2 pouches. Drizzle a little olive oil over the beets and sprinkle with some coarse salt. Wrap them completely in the foil. Place the foil pouch(es) on a baking sheet and cook for 30 minutes. Once the beets are cooked, remove from the oven and foil, and let cool for 10 minutes, or until cool enough to handle. Peel and cut them into thin wedges or slices.

3 Place the leeks, onions, shallots, golden raisins and green onions in a roasting pan and drizzle with some olive oil, a good pinch of salt and some pepper. Roast in the oven for 20 minutes, turning the mixture once or twice. Add the cooked beets to the roasting pan and cook for another 5 minutes.

4 Pour a little olive oil into a separate pan placed over medium heat. Add the snap peas, English peas, spinach and chives and cook for 3-4 minutes or until the spinach has wilted.

5 Place all of the vegetables from the oven and the pan into a salad bowl, toss to combine. Add some lemon juice and a drizzle of olive oil. Salt and pepper to taste, toss once more, *et voila!*

Raw Beet and Goat Cheese Salad

I am very, very fond of goat cheese. If I had to, I could possibly give up other cheeses, but goat cheese? Now that would be a challenge. I particularly like slightly creamy, young goat cheese with an ash rind, such as a Valençay or a Selles-Sur-Cher. You can imagine my delight, therefore, when I spied a similar type of cheese in my local farmers' market in Santa Barbara, California. The cheese, made by Drake Family Farm, was the perfect foil for the beautiful golden and Chioggia beets I had found in the market that day too. This salad is the result of pairing the two — I love the balance the cheese gives to the pepperiness of the raw beets.

Serves 8 people

For the salad:

6–8 yellow beets — peeled and thinly sliced, on a mandolin if possible

6–8 Chioggia beets — peeled and thinly sliced, on a mandolin if possible

8 oz ash covered goat cheese or a goat cheese log — sliced as thinly as possible

¼ cup packed small mint leaves

2 tablespoons thinly sliced chives

For the vinaigrette:

¼ cup olive oil

Zest and juice of 1 lemon

Pinch of salt

5–6 grinds of black pepper

1 Arrange the beet slices in concentric circles over eight dinner plates, alternating between the yellow and Chioggia disks. Insert the goat cheese pieces between every second or third beet slice.

2 Tuck the mint leaves between slices and scatter the chives over each plate.

3 In a small bowl, whisk the vinaigrette ingredients together to form a smooth emulsion. Pour the vinaigrette over the beets at least 5 minutes before serving.

Movers and Shakers Salad

My longtime friend, local businesswoman and entrepreneur Anne Bloodgood Pazier runs Santa Barbara Gift Baskets. Her company showcases many products from local manufacturers. I am thrilled that my books and spice line have been part of her lineup for many years. She also has a gift: that of community builder and networking superstar. This summer she invited the owners of the companies whose products she features, to a gathering she named, "Makers, Bakers, Movers and Shakers," because, as she told us on the day, "that's who you all are!" The potluck brunch proved to be a brainstorming-chin-wagging-inspiring mind fest. I made this salad as my contribution to the brunch, and have named it after all the incredible women it is my privilege to work with. Thank you, ladies!

Serves 8 people

For the salad:

4 yellow beets

4 Chioggia beets

Olive oil

Salt

Black pepper

1 lb assorted cherry tomatoes — quartered

1 head baby gem lettuce — leaves separated

3 white nectarines — halved, pitted and sliced

3 green onions — finely sliced

1/2 cup packed small mint leaves

1/4 cup packed basil leaves

1 small zucchini — entirely peeled into long thin strips

For the vinaigrette:

3 tablespoons olive oil

1 tablespoon Dijon mustard

1 tablespoon white wine vinegar

Pinch of salt

8–10 grinds of black pepper

1 Preheat the oven to 350 degrees.

2 Place the unpeeled beets in a small baking dish. Drizzle with olive oil, add a good pinch of salt and 5–6 grinds of pepper, and roast for 50–60 minutes, or until tender when pierced with a knife. When cool enough to handle, peel the beets and cut into thin wedges or slices.

3 Pour the vinaigrette ingredients into a large salad bowl and whisk together well. Place salad utensils on top of the vinaigrette.

4 Arrange the sliced beets and all the remaining salad ingredients in the salad bowl. Toss the salad well when ready to serve.

CARROTS

Rainbow Carrot
Salad

—

Sautéed Purple Kale
and Carrot Salad

—

Moroccan Carrot
Salad with Golden
Raisins

—

Roasted Kale and
Rainbow Carrot
Salad

—

Carrot, Radish and
Orange Salad

Rainbow Carrot Salad

This is a jazzed-up version of the simplest of salads, one I used to eat in France as a small child, *salade de carottes râpées*, basically, grated carrots, lemon juice and olive oil. My grandmother made this salad for my brother and me all the time, and we have fond memories of it to this day. It's also ubiquitous bistro fare, a simple national dish that anyone growing up in France knows well. American food writer and Parisian transplant, David Lebowitz, wrote a blog post about this salad stating that one should refrain from messing about with the original. However, when I spied these rather extraordinary, elegantly tapered, multi-colored carrots at the market, I couldn't resist a little tinkering with the recipe. I like to think my lovely grandmother would have approved; I know my brother does!

Serves 8 people

2 lbs fresh, assorted multi-colored carrots — peeled and grated (use the largest holes on a box grater)

¼ cup olive oil

Juice and zest of 2–3 lemons

2 tablespoons finely chopped parsley

⅓ cup toasted pine nuts

8 dates (Barhi or Medjool if possible) — pitted and chopped

Sea salt

Black pepper

1 Place the carrots in a large salad bowl. Drizzle the olive oil and lemon juice over the carrots. Sprinkle the lemon zest, parsley, pine nuts and dates over the carrots and add a generous pinch of salt and 7–8 grinds of pepper.

2 Toss well to combine, at least 10 minutes before serving.

Sautéed Purple Kale and Carrot Salad

I am often asked where I get my culinary inspiration from, and the answer, more often than not is, "from whatever I come across at the market." There is also an old adage, "You eat with your eyes first," and that is precisely what happened when I found this stunning purple chidori kale. I could see the farmer's table piled high with these frilly, striated leaves from two aisles away, so intense was their color. I leaped across, zigzagging my way through the crowds at top speed, lest they got whisked away, and scooped up a huge bagful. I also happened upon some carrots of the same startling color that day. The ingredients for this dish literally came together in my basket as I meandered through the market. This is truly one of my favorite ways to compose dishes.

Serves 8

For the salad:

Olive oil

1/2 lb baby chidori kale — any thick stalks removed

1 lb purple, white and yellow carrots — quartered lengthwise if they are large, and cut into 2-inch long pieces

1 teaspoon za'atar

Salt

Black pepper

1 lb (8–10) small globe white turnips — cleaned, peeled if the outer skin is rough, and thinly sliced

1/2 cup packed small mint leaves

For the vinaigrette:

2 tablespoons olive oil

4 green (spring) onions — ends trimmed, then very finely sliced

1 teaspoon black sesame seeds

1 teaspoon toasted sesame oil

Zest and juice of 1 lemon

1 tablespoon white wine vinegar of Champagne vinegar

1 Pour 1 tablespoons olive oil into a large skillet placed over medium-high heat. Add the kale and cook, stirring frequently for 3–4 minutes. The kale should be just wilted. Place the kale on a large serving platter or divide among eight salad plates.

2 Return the same skillet to the heat, and add 1 tablespoon olive oil, the sliced carrots, za'atar, a good pinch of salt and 4–5 grinds of black pepper. Cook the carrots for 4–5 minutes, stirring frequently. They will still be crunchy. Scatter the carrots on top of the kale. Set the skillet aside.

3 Tuck the turnip slices into the salad, then sprinkle the mint leaves over the top.

4 To make the vinaigrette, pour the olive oil into the skillet, placed over medium heat. Add the sliced green onions and sauté for 1–2 minutes until just golden. Add the remaining vinaigrette ingredients and stir to combine. Pour the warm vinaigrette over the salad and serve.

Moroccan Carrot Salad with Golden Raisins

Morocco is known for its scented, flavorful cuisine, for its judicious use of spices and the layering of flavors within each dish. This carrot salad was inspired by some sweet, yellow carrots I found at the market along with some golden flame raisins. The raisins were huge, almost honey filled. We munched on them as we walked around the market picking up some of the other ingredients for dinner. I served this with a roasted chicken that had been cooked with Ras al Hanout and preserved lemons.

Serves 8 people

Olive oil

10–12 yellow carrots — peeled and thinly sliced

6 shallots — peeled, halved and thinly sliced

2 tablespoons golden raisins

1 pinch saffron threads

1 pinch cumin powder

Coarse sea salt and black pepper

Lemon olive oil

Zest of 1 lemon

1 small bunch cilantro leaves

2 tablespoons chives — finely chopped

1 Pour a little olive oil into a large pan placed over medium heat. Toss the carrots, shallots and golden raisins in the pan and coat with the oil. Sprinkle in the saffron and cumin and stir all the ingredients together. Cook for 8–10 minutes stirring frequently. The shallots should be soft and translucent, just barely cooked, and the saffron should be just releasing its fragrance.

2 Transfer the carrot-shallot mixture to a salad bowl. Drizzle with a little lemon olive oil, add a dash of salt and some black pepper, the lemon zest, chives and the cilantro leaves. Toss well to combine. I like serving this in small individual tagines, alongside a main course or as part of a series of small plates, tapas style.

Roasted Kale and Rainbow Carrot Salad

This salad is from a spring blog post of mine. I came across some sensational-looking rainbow carrots at the market and have been trying out all sorts of dishes with them. I've steamed them, roasted them, grated and chopped them. I love their color and really wanted to retain that in the finished dish. I found that if you cook the carrots for a short amount of time, they still retain some of their crunchiness and are visually very appetizing. Combine that with the earthy overtones of roasted kale, and you have the makings of a beautiful and very healthy salad. The great thing about this dish is that you can use any kind of kale. In fact, it's all the more appealing if you can find some purple kale and combine it with one of the curly green varieties. Kale is really easy to cook. All this salad needs is 10 minutes in the oven, and it's done. This salad can be prepped hours in advance and then popped into the oven at the last minute. I asked my kids to help prepare the carrots; they loved making the carrot ribbons.

Serves 8 people

2 lbs rainbow carrots — washed

2 lbs kale — different types — roughly chopped

Olive oil to drizzle, plus 1/4 cup olive oil

Sea salt and black pepper

1 tablespoon fig balsamic vinegar

Zest and juice of 1 orange

Pinch of sumac

1 Preheat the oven to 350 degrees.

2 Using a vegetable peeler, peel the carrots into thin shavings. Place the carrot shavings and the kale into a large bowl and drizzle with a little olive oil, sprinkle with a large pinch of salt and 8–10 grinds of pepper. Toss to coat well and then mound all the vegetables onto one sheet pan. They will be piled high — which is okay.

3 Roast the vegetables for 10 minutes.

4 While the vegetables are cooking, prepare the vinaigrette. Combine 1/4 cup olive oil, the vinegar, sumac, orange zest and juice, a pinch of salt and some freshly ground pepper in the bottom of a large salad bowl and whisk together. Set aside.

5 When the vegetables are ready, remove from the oven and add to the salad bowl. Toss well to coat with the vinaigrette.

Carrot, Radish and Orange Salad

Suddenly, there are versions of this salad everywhere. This is my take on this crunchy, juicy and peppery salad. You can use blood oranges when they are in season and different varieties of radishes for a little variation.

Serves 8 people

For the salad:

4 oranges — peeled and thinly sliced into disks

4 carrots — peeled and very thinly sliced

8–10 radishes — washed and thinly sliced

2 tablespoons finely chopped chives

For the vinaigrette:

¼ cup olive oil

Juice of ½ lemon

1 teaspoon orange flower water

1 pinch cumin

1 pinch cinnamon

Large pinch of sea salt

6–7 grinds of black pepper

1 Place the sliced oranges, carrots and radishes on a platter and arrange them in an appealing pattern.

2 In a small bowl, whisk the vinaigrette ingredients together to form a smooth emulsion.

3 Pour the vinaigrette over the oranges and then sprinkle with the chives a good 10 minutes before you serve the salad.

ENDIVE & FENNEL

Endive and
Microgreen Salad

—

Summer Salad

—

Endive, Asparagus
and Burrata Salad

—

Fennel, Endive and
Walnut Salad

—

Fennel, Endive and
Smoked Salmon
Salad

—

Santa Barbara Red
Rock Crab with a
Shaved Fennel Salad

—

Endive and Fig Salad

—

Shaved Fennel and
Radish Salad

Endive and Microgreen Salad

I took my daughter to Thomas Keller's Bouchon Bistro in Los Angeles for her sixteenth birthday. She was thrilled; so was I. The bistro resembles a large Parisian brasserie, shades of Lipp or La Coupole, complete with high vaulted ceilings, tiled floors and waiters gliding around with starched calf-length white aprons. The menu is classic bistro fare. The chef had a salad on the menu that was his play on the classic endive-walnut-blue cheese combination, using big chunks of blue cheese, whole toasted walnuts and both red and white Belgian endives that were stacked in an appealing manner. This dish is inspired by that visit.

Serves 8 people

5 tablespoons olive oil

1 tablespoon sherry vinegar

Sea salt

Black pepper

Juice and zest of 1 lemon

6 endives — cored and leaves left whole

1 apple — a sweet crunchy one — peeled, cored and thinly sliced

3–4 oz microgreens

4 oz pistachios or almonds or a mixture of both — roughly chopped

6 oz feta cheese (optional)

1 Combine the olive oil, vinegar, lemon zest and juice, a pinch of salt and 5–6 grinds of pepper in a large bowl and whisk together vigorously. Place the endive leaves and apples in the bowl and toss very gently. The endive leaves can be a little delicate.

2 Divide the endives and apples between eight plates and stack them in a cross-hatch pattern. Sprinkle each plate with some of the microgreens and the nuts. Grind some black pepper and crumble the cheese on top.

Summer Salad

My good friend Sherry arrived at my house one day with three ears of beautiful, just-picked corn. It really did not need cooking at all as the kernels were so sweet and juicy. We chopped up a bunch of other vegetables so that they were all kernel-size and made a quick summer salad. You can make the same salad with grilled corn, which I also like, bringing some of the char-grilled flavors to the mix.

Serves 8 people

1 tablespoon Dijon mustard

4 tablespoons olive oil

1 tablespoon white wine vinegar

Sea salt and black pepper

3 ears fresh corn — try to find the multi-colored type if you can

4 small Belgian endives — leaves removed and left whole

1 small-medium daikon radish — diced

1 green apple — peeled, cored and diced

1/2 English cucumber — peeled and diced

2 tablespoons chives — finely diced

1 tablespoon chopped dill — finely diced

1 Combine the mustard, olive oil, vinegar, a good pinch of salt and some pepper in the bottom of a large bowl.

2 Steam the corn for 4–5 minutes. Remove from the stove and shuck the corn. Place the kernels into the bowl with the vinaigrette.

3 Add all the remaining ingredients and toss together well, taking care with the endive leaves as they can be a little delicate.

Endive, Asparagus and Burrata Salad

Earlier this year, I had the pleasure of celebrating a very special Sunday lunch with a large group of friends and family. It was a transcontinental, multi-cultural, multi-ethnic gathering, with smatterings of different languages ebbing back and forth over the huge table as everyone got to know one another. It was a beautiful, laughter-filled, languorous afternoon, where everyone took time to listen to each other's stories. I love meals like this, where good conversations abound, and no one is in any hurry to leave.

I got a little carried away making a multitude of dishes for the occasion, including an array of salads. This is one of my favorites from that day.

Serves 8 people

For the salad:

5–6 Belgian endives — cored and leaves left whole

1 lb thick stemmed asparagus — tips left whole, stalks entirely peeled into long strips

2 whole burrata — carefully quartered

2 packed cups basil leaves

For the vinaigrette:

3 tablespoons lemon olive oil

Zest and juice of 1 lemon

2 teaspoons pear Champagne vinegar or white wine vinegar

Coarse sea salt

Black pepper

1 Arrange the endive leaves around the sides and across the bottom of a large serving plate. Place the asparagus strips over the endive leaves in the middle of the plate. Scatter the basil leaves over the vegetables, then carefully place the pieces of burrata on top.

2 In a small bowl, whisk together the vinaigrette ingredients to form a smooth emulsion. Add a generous pinch of salt and 7–8 grinds of black pepper. Whisk again. When ready to serve, pour the vinaigrette over the salad.

Fennel, Endive and Walnut Salad

Endive and blue cheese are a natural food pairing, akin to port and Stilton or Sauternes and Roquefort. I think that fennel and blue cheese fall into that same category. Here, the vegetables are combined with herbs and nuts for a rustic, fresh, crisp salad.

Serves 8 people

1 rounded tablespoon Dijon mustard

¼ cup olive oil

2 tablespoons vinegar — such as apple bouquet vinegar or Jerez vinegar

Sea salt and black pepper

1 large fennel bulb — cut in half and thinly sliced

3 endives — cut in half and thinly sliced

3 apples — choose a crunchy variety that is a little sweet such as Gala — cut into thin slices

8 oz mache greens

4 oz nuts — walnuts, cashews or pistachios or a mix — roughly chopped

4 oz golden raisins

6 oz blue cheese — such as Fourme d'Ambert or other variety of mild blue cheese

2 tablespoons parsley — finely chopped

1 tablespoon chives — finely chopped

2 tablespoons small mint leaves — left whole (if the leaves are large, cut them in half)

1 Place the mustard in a large salad bowl. Drizzle in the olive oil and whisk until you have a thick vinaigrette with the consistency of mayonnaise. Add the vinegar in the same manner. Taste and season with a little salt and pepper.

2 Place salad servers over the vinaigrette and then place all the salad ingredients on top of the salad servers, ensuring that the ingredients do not fall into the vinaigrette. When you are ready to serve the salad, toss it gently so that everything is well combined.

Fennel, Endive and Smoked Salmon Salad

I really like good smoked salmon. It's one of those foods that I rarely get tired of, be it on toast with a squeeze of lemon, with a poached egg, with scrambled eggs, in a soufflé, in a sandwich, on a flatbread or on a pizza. I'm beginning to sound like Sam I Am and his green eggs and ham, but there are really very few things that I would not eat smoked salmon with. Adding salmon to salads lends a certain elegance and richness to the dish. I love it every time.

Serves 8 people

¼ cup pistachios — roughly chopped

¼ cup olive oil

1 tablespoon red wine vinegar

Sea salt and black pepper

4 endives — halved and thinly sliced crosswise

1 large fennel bulb — fronds trimmed, quartered and thinly sliced crosswise

2 large handfuls mesclun salad mix

1 tablespoon olives— finely sliced

8 oz smoked salmon — cut into thin strips

2 tablespoons dill — finely chopped

¼ cup parsley — finely chopped

1 bunch chives — finely chopped

1 Place a heavy-bottomed pan over medium heat. When the pan is hot, add the pistachios and dry roast them for 2–3 minutes. Remove the pan from the heat and add the olive oil and vinegar. Whisk together well. Pour the vinaigrette with the nuts into the bottom of a large salad bowl. Add a pinch of salt and some black pepper. Place serving utensils over the vinaigrette.

2 Place the remaining ingredients on top of the utensils. When you are ready to serve the salad, toss it gently so that everything is well combined.

NOTE: If you don't have smoked salmon, you can substitute cooked salmon filet.

Santa Barbara Red Rock Crab with a Shaved Fennel Salad

I once taught a class with a dynamic young woman who used to wholesale fish. She would work directly with the local fishermen so her product literally came straight off the boat. She called me one day and said she had some great local crab. This is the salad we made together. The avocado vinaigrette is buttery and works wonders with the crab and fennel.

Serves 8 people

For the crab:

16 crab claws

1 tablespoon chopped chives

1 lemon — cut into 8 wedges

For the vinaigrette:

$1/4$ cup olive oil

1 tablespoon apple cider
    vinegar or Champagne
    vinegar

1 avocado — peeled and the
    meat scooped out

1 tablespoon lemon juice

Pinch of sea salt and black
    pepper

1 tablespoon freshly
    chopped parsley

For the fennel salad:

2 whole fennel bulbs —
    cut in half lengthwise
    and very thinly sliced

1 lemon — zested and then
    quartered

1 tablespoon fresh dill —
    finely chopped

1 small green apple — cored
    and very thinly sliced

1 tablespoon chives —
    finely chopped

Flake salt

1 Steam the crab claws for 15–18 minutes.

2 Place some newspaper on a counter or table. Remove the crab claws from the steamer and place on the newspaper. Lay each claw flat on the paper. Hold the claw with a dishcloth and use a mallet to firmly crack open the shell. Extricate the crab meat.

3 For the vinaigrette, pour the olive oil into a small bowl and whisk in the vinegar. Add the avocado meat and mash with a fork. Add the lemon juice, parsley, salt and 2–3 grinds of pepper and whisk with the fork so that all the ingredients form a homogeneous vinaigrette.

4 Place the fennel, lemon zest, dill, apples and chives into a medium-sized bowl and toss with the vinaigrette.

5 To serve, place a spoonful of the fennel salad in the center of each plate, and then place the crab meat on top. Add a little salt and pepper, a sprinkling of freshly chopped chives, a squeeze of fresh lemon juice and serve immediately.

Endive and Fig Salad

I have written about my neighbor's fig tree before. It literally drips with figs. Every time I walk past the tree, I am so, so tempted to pluck one from the overhanging branches, but have resisted temptation. Instead, I rely on the beautiful figs from the farmers' market. I love sweet figs and slightly bitter endives together; they make a great salad. You can make this salad with or without cheese. I found that goat cheese, feta or Queso de Valdeón work well.

Serves 8 to 10 people

For the endives:

1/2 bunch cilantro leaves

3 tablespoons olive oil

1 tablespoon lemon juice

Pinch of coarse sea salt

6 large Belgian endives — cut in half and leaves removed from the core but left whole

For the fig salad:

3 tablespoons olive oil

1 tablespoon apple cider vinegar

2 pints assorted figs — each fig cut into eighths

4 Asian pears — peeled and thinly sliced

3 green onions — very thinly sliced

4 oz baby arugula

4 oz Queso de Valdeón — crumbled (optional)

1 Combine the cilantro, olive oil, lemon juice and salt in the bottom of a large bowl and whisk together. Place salad servers over the vinaigrette and add the endive leaves.

2 When ready to assemble the salad, remove the salad utensils and let the endive leaves fall into the vinaigrette, then very gently toss the leaves. You want them to remain whole and not bruise.

3 Arrange 10–12 of the endive leaves on a salad plate in the shape of a flower so that the root end of each leaf is in the center of the plate. Repeat with each of the eight plates.

4 For the fig salad, pour the olive oil and apple cider vinegar into a large bowl and whisk together. Place serving utensils over the vinaigrette. Place all the remaining ingredients on top of the utensils, except for the cheese.

5 After you have prepared the plates with the endive flowers and are ready to serve the salad, carefully toss the fig salad. Divide it equally into eight portions. Mound it in the center of each of the endive flowers. Crumble the cheese on top of each salad.

Shaved Fennel and Radish Salad

This is a simple, yet very elegant, crisp and refreshing salad. It's also quick and easy to prepare. I particularly like to serve this alongside grilled or roasted fish, or as part of a vegetarian feast.

Serves 8 people

For the salad:

4 medium-sized fennel bulbs — thinly sliced, lengthwise, on a mandolin if possible

10 radishes — ends trimmed then thinly sliced

4 oz crumbled feta

2 tablespoons finely chopped dill

For the vinaigrette:

1/4 cup olive oil

Zest and juice 1 lemon

2 teaspoons white wine vinegar or Champagne vinegar

Large pinch of sea salt

6–7 grinds of black pepper

1 Place the fennel slices, side by side in a concentric pattern, on a large serving platter. You will not use all of the slices to cover the platter; place any remaining fennel slices to the center of the platter. Arrange the radishes on top of the fennel. Scatter the feta and dill over the top.

2 In a small bowl, whisk the vinaigrette ingredients together to form a smooth emulsion. Pour the vinaigrette over the salad when ready to serve.

FIGS

Fig and Frisée Salad

—

Fig Tapenade Crostini
with a Watercress
Salad

—

Fig, Grape and
Ricotta Salad

—

Fig and Prosciutto
Salad

—

Fig and Tomato
Salad with Purple
Basil

—

Fig and Melon
Salad

Fig and Frisée Salad

Elizabeth David, the marvelously eloquent British cookery writer once wrote, "To eat figs off the tree in the very early morning, when they have been barely touched by the sun, is one of the exquisite pleasures of the Mediterranean." I feel exactly the same way when I find figs at the market for the first time in the summer, and bite into the first succulent mouthful. Ripe figs are sweetly deceptive. Behind their plain covers, albeit ones with beautiful aubergine and sometimes chartreuse coloring, lie hidden treasures; nature's honey scented poetry enveloped in a small, plum-sized case. This salad celebrates that poetry with a veritable fig "tree."

Serves 8 people

For the salad:

1 head frisée lettuce

1 head red leaf lettuce

4 oz assorted microgreens — I like to use a mixture of onion, daikon and radish microgreens

6–8 figs — quartered

For the vinaigrette:

3 tablespoons olive oil

Zest and juice of 1 lemon

2 teaspoons of fig balsamic vinegar or red wine vinegar

1 pinch of coarse sea salt

6–7 grinds of black pepper

1 Cover a large serving platter with the different varieties of lettuce, interspersing the leaves with small tufts of microgreens. Fan out the quartered fig pieces over the greens.

2 In a small bowl, whisk together all the vinaigrette ingredients to form an emulsion. When ready to serve, pour the vinaigrette over the salad.

Fig Tapenade Crostini with a Watercress Salad

This is what you make when you either have too many figs or too many ripe figs. Olives and figs are oddly wonderful together — it's that whole salty-sweet thing that works so well. You can also serve the crostini as an appetizer.

Serves 8 people

For the crostini:

1 cup black olives — pitted

1 teaspoon capers

1 clove garlic — chopped

Juice and zest of 1 lemon

8–10 fresh figs

Olive oil

Baguette or ciabatta — cut into thin slices and toasted

1/2 bunch chives — finely chopped

For the salad:

3 tablespoons olive oil

Juice of 1 lemon

Sea salt and black pepper

4–6 oz watercress (use some watercress microgreens too, if you can find them)

24 small green figs — halved

1 Place the olives, capers, garlic, lemon juice and zest and 8–10 figs in a food processor and pulse until you have a coarse tapenade.

2 Drizzle a little olive oil onto each slice of toast and spoon some of the tapenade onto the toasts. Sprinkle the tops of each crostini with some of the chopped chives.

3 For the watercress salad, whisk the olive oil and lemon juice together in a small bowl. Season with a little salt and pepper.

4 Divide the watercress greens between eight plates and arrange the rest of the figs on top of the greens. Drizzle with the vinaigrette. Place 2 or 3 crostini onto each plate and serve.

Fig, Grape and Ricotta Salad

I had planned to make a fig and buffalo mozzarella salad for dinner. You know, the one where you slowly tear pieces of fresh mozzarella apart, pop it on a plate, add some figs and drizzle with a little olive oil. That was the plan, until my lovely friend Nancy arrived with some truly incredible seedless grapes from her garden. She and her husband have magic soil and produce sumptuous veggies and fruit. The grapes were bursting with flavor and were sweet and juicy. I decided I had to add them to the salad too, along with these crunchy, slightly salty, blistered almonds I picked up at the farmers' market. If you can get your hands on the blistered almonds from Fat Uncle Farms — do. They are incredible.

I had intended to pick up the mozzarella but got completely sidetracked by the fresh ricotta I spied in the cheese shop. Um... fresh ricotta with figs, the grapes, the almonds and some arugula for a little zing in the salad. Ricotta in hand, I rushed home and made this salad. I've made it with crumbled feta cheese, which works well, too. Both versions are yummy.

Serves 8 people

4 oz arugula

32 figs — quartered

1 bunch grapes — halved

3 oz salted almonds

1/2 lb fresh ricotta

Zest and juice of 2 lemons

1 tablespoon honey

5 tablespoons olive oil

Sea salt and black pepper

1 Divide the arugula between eight dinner plates. Scatter the figs, grapes and almonds over the arugula. Dot the top of each salad with some of the fresh ricotta.

2 Combine the lemon zest and juice, honey, olive oil, a pinch of salt and 4–5 grinds of fresh black pepper in a small bowl and whisk together vigorously. You want the honey to be completely incorporated into the other ingredients, otherwise it just tends to sit at the bottom of the bowl. When you are ready to serve, pour a little of the vinaigrette over each plate.

Fig and Prosciutto Salad

This is one of the salads I usually make as soon as I get back to my father's house in France. One of the first things I do there is to go to the market. By market, I mean one that takes place outdoors and not a shop. This market takes place twice a week, on Tuesday and Saturday mornings in a bucolic, tree-lined square. It is one of my all-time favorite places to be. I love meandering through the colorful aisles, feasting on all the delicacies. I'll pick up olives, tapenade, some bread, such as *fougasse* and *pain aux noix*; a sampling of fresh goat cheese, made in the previous 48 hours, from what has to be the best cheese shop on wheels in Provence; and some prosciutto. This is prosciutto that melts in your mouth. It is very hard not to polish off the entire carefully-wrapped package before I get home — particularly, as I also have that just-baked, slightly warm piece of bread in my basket. Add to this some vegetables and fruit, and we're ready for lunch. I'll make a small green salad to go with this, eat some of the goat cheese and munch on the bread. This is my idea of the perfect day.

Serves 8 people

16 ripe figs — some left whole, some halved, some quartered

16 slices prosciutto

4 oz olives — pitted, left whole

1 small bunch chives — finely chopped

4 oz Manchego — shaved into thin slices

Large handful basil leaves

Sea salt and black pepper

3 tablespoons olive oil

1 tablespoon red wine vinegar

1 Arrange the prosciutto on a large serving platter. Dot the surface of the prosciutto with the figs and olives. Sprinkle the chives over the top.

2 Add the Manchego shavings, the basil leaves, a pinch of salt and some pepper.

3 Combine the olive oil and vinegar in a small bowl and whisk together well. Drizzle the vinaigrette over the salad and serve.

Fig and Tomato Salad with Purple Basil

This salad came about one day when, for no particular reason, I sliced figs horizontally instead of in the more traditional quarters. All these exquisite ruby-colored fig disks were strewn on my cutting board. I sliced some tomatoes in the same manner and arranged them on a plate, drizzled some olive oil over the top, added a couple of purple basil leaves from the garden and sat down to lunch. This salad, along with the peach and tomato salad, are now two of my summer favorites.

Serves 8 people

1 lb assorted tomatoes

1 basket figs — assorted if possible (smile sweetly at the farmer and he might create a mixed basket for you)

1 bunch purple basil leaves

A good fruity olive oil

Coarse sea salt

Black pepper

1 Carefully wash all the tomatoes and figs. The larger tomatoes should be handled with care as they can bruise easily.

2 Using a serrated knife or a very sharp knife, slice the tomatoes horizontally. Arrange them on a dinner plate, mixing the varieties and colors so that they cover the entire surface.

3 Prepare the figs. Cut each fig into thin slices, the same way you sliced the tomatoes. This creates a great looking pattern.

4 Carefully insert the assorted fig slices between the tomato slices.

5 Insert the whole basil leaves between the fruit and then drizzle a little olive oil over the entire salad. Sprinkle some coarse sea salt and grind some black pepper over the entire dish.

Fig and Melon Salad

Food, like music, has the peculiar ability to transport you to another time and place. If I hear the first licks of "California Girls" by the Beach Boys, I instantly see my young pre-teen self, sitting in the back of my parents' convertible, top down, belting out the lyrics to the music being played on a clunky 8-track tape deck. It's the summertime, the air is warm, the light golden and I have few cares in the world. Ah, the joys of summer!

I have the same reaction when I come across Charentais or Cavaillon melons, whose heady violet, jasmine perfume permeates the air of any market stand. That aroma holds the promise of the taste of luscious, honeyed apricots, and evokes, for me, the image of picnics in Provence. You can imagine my delight therefore, when tasting a local Tuscan-style cantaloupe melon in the farmers' market in California, I felt I had just stepped into the South of France. Needless to say, I brought some home and made this salad; an ode to the sweet taste of summer.

Serves 8 people

For the salad:

2 Tuscan melons — halved, seeds removed and flesh scooped out with a spoon

16 assorted figs — quartered

$1/3$ cup raw pistachios

$1/3$ cup mint leaves

2 oz goat cheese — crumbled into small pieces

1 tablespoon finely chopped chives

For the vinaigrette:

3 tablespoons fruity olive oil

Zest and juice of 1 lemon

1 tablespoon balsamic vinegar

1 pinch of coarse sea salt

8–10 grinds of black pepper

1 Place the melon scoops and figs in a salad bowl. Scatter the pistachios, mint leaves, goat cheese and chives over the top.

2 In a small bowl, whisk together all the vinaigrette ingredients to form an emulsion. Pour over the salad just before serving and toss to combine.

GRAINS & RICE

Couscous Salad

~

Cauliflower, Quinoa
and Herb Salad

~

Watercress Tabbouleh

~

Forbidden Rice with
Grilled Brussels
Sprouts

~

Red Quinoa with
Blood Oranges,
Pistachios, Herbs
and Thyme-Encrusted
Roasted Duck Legs

~

Multicolored
Quinoa Salad with
Roasted Portobello
Mushrooms

~

Multi-Rice and
Zucchini Salad

Couscous Salad

Thought to have originated in North Africa, couscous — which is made from rolling semolina (the heart of durum wheat) into a fine grain — is one of the traditional dishes of Morocco, Tunisia and Algeria. It's usually cooked with vegetables and some meat, herbs and a variety of spices. As couscous has become more widely available and easier to prepare, its popularity has spread worldwide.

I like to use couscous in salads and incorporate the herbs, fruits and vegetables I have on hand. If apricots are not in season, you can use dried apricots or peaches instead. You can also use different herbs such as parsley or cilantro. Couscous is a wonderful picnic food.

Serves 8 people

3 tablespoons olive oil

2 cups couscous (uncooked)

1 red onion — peeled and thinly sliced

1/3 cup dried cranberries or dried cherries

1 large bunch chives — finely chopped

1/4 cup pistachios — chopped

Zest of 1 lemon

1 tablespoon red wine vinegar

Large pinch of sea salt

10–12 grinds of black pepper

6 apricots — each cut into 8 pieces

1 Bring 2 cups salted water and 1 tablespoon olive oil to a boil in a large saucepan. Add the couscous, cover, remove from the heat and let sit for 10 minutes. Remove the lid and fluff the couscous with a fork.

2 While the couscous is cooking, pour a little olive oil into a medium-sized skillet placed over medium heat. Add the red onion and dried cranberries and sauté until soft and translucent — about 4 minutes. Stir in the chives, pistachios and lemon zest, and cook for 1 minute more. Remove from the heat.

3 Combine the remaining olive oil, vinegar, salt and pepper in the bottom of a medium-sized salad bowl. Add the red onion mixture to the vinaigrette and toss to combine. Add the cooked couscous and the chopped apricots. Carefully toss the salad so that the apricots do not get squished.

Cauliflower, Quinoa and Herb Salad

Like kale and Brussels sprouts, cauliflower has become the vegetable "du jour." Magazine articles herald its many uses, restaurants make a feature of whole baked heads, and it has exploded in the gluten-free, keto mania world. Often thought to be a boring cousin of broccoli, cauliflower is enjoying a culinary renaissance.

Long a staple in our house in dishes such as gratins, soups and purées, I had never really used it raw, except in a platter of crudités. After discovering its sweet-nutty flavor and subtle al dente texture when grated, I thought I'd try it in a tabbouleh-esque salad. This is the herbaceous-filled result, and now, one of my favorite salads.

Serves 8 people

For the salad:

1 cup red quinoa — thoroughly rinsed

1 cup vegetable stock

1 large cauliflower — florets separated and grated, either on a box grater or in a food processor

1 cup finely chopped parsley

1 cup finely chopped cilantro

1/2 cup finely chopped chives

1/2 cup finely chopped mint

1/2 cup sesame seeds

1/2 cup chopped pistachios

Salt

Black pepper

For the vinaigrette:

1/4 cup olive oil

Juice of 2 Meyer lemons

2 tablespoons sesame oil

1 Place the quinoa in a saucepan with the vegetable stock and bring to a boil. Reduce to a simmer, cover and cook until the quinoa has absorbed all the liquid. You can also cook the quinoa in a rice cooker, using the same proportions. Once cooked, fluff with a fork and let cool.

2 In a large salad bowl combine the cooled quinoa, cauliflower, parsley, cilantro, chives and mint. Be sure to mix well so that the ingredients are evenly distributed throughout the salad.

3 Place the sesame seeds and pistachios in a medium-sized skillet placed over medium heat. Dry roast in the pan about 1–2 minutes, until just fragrant. Add to the salad and stir to combine.

4 In a small bowl, whisk together the olive oil, lemon juice and sesame oil to form an emulsion. Pour over the cauliflower mixture. Season with a good pinch of salt and 10–12 grinds of pepper, and combine thoroughly. Serve at room temperature.

Watercress Tabbouleh

Purists would give me a hard time calling this dish tabbouleh, which is traditionally made with bulgur, has tomatoes and cucumber in it and is filled with masses of herbs. My interpretation is made with couscous grains instead of bulgur, and with lots of watercress plus a few spices and some dates. Not traditional, but yummy nonetheless.

The original versions stem from Lebanon and Syria, where couscous is usually part of the *mezze* (appetizer) table. It's really a herb salad with a little bit of bulgur added. This version is half and half. If you prefer the bright green herb salad, use half the quantity of couscous (or bulgur) and increase the amount of herbs.

Serves 8 people

1 cup water

1 cup couscous (you can also make this with fine bulgur, although the preparation of the bulgur is slightly different)

1 tablespoon butter

Large pinch of sea salt

1 large red onion — peeled and finely chopped

1 teaspoon cumin

1/2 teaspoon ground cardamom

3 bunches watercress leaves — finely sliced

1 large bunch fresh mint leaves — finely sliced

1 large bunch chives — finely chopped

1/2 bunch parsley — finely chopped

1 medium-sized yellow tomato — finely diced

Juice and zest of 2 lemons

1/3 cup olive oil

Sea salt and black pepper

1 In a large saucepan, bring the water to a boil. Add the couscous, salt and butter; cover and remove from the heat. Leave covered for 10 minutes. Remove the lid and fluff the couscous with a fork. Transfer the cooked couscous to a bowl.

2 While the couscous is cooking, pour a little olive oil into a medium-sized skillet placed over medium heat. Add the finely diced red onion, the cumin and cardamom and cook, stirring frequently, until the onions are completely soft, about 8–10 minutes. Add the onions to the cooked couscous.

3 When the couscous and onion mixture has cooled to room temperature, stir in the herbs. When you are ready to serve the couscous, sprinkle it with the lemon juice, add the olive oil, some salt and pepper, and toss.

Forbidden Rice with Grilled Brussels Sprouts

Ah, forbidden rice. Ancient Chinese legend has it that if you were caught eating black rice you would face severe consequences, as this was the food of the Emperor's court. Thankfully, we can now all partake of this delicious nutty rice without fear of losing our heads. Black rice turns an incredible deep, deep purple color when cooked. It's packed with antioxidants and anthocyanins, so it's good for you, but most of all, it's really rather delicious.

About Brussels sprouts: When I lived in London, there was a Scottish woman who lived in the ground-floor flat beneath ours. She "killed" vegetables on an almost daily basis, literally boiling them to death for hours on end, voiding them of any nutritional value at all. The worst days were when she cooked cabbage or Brussels sprouts. The extraordinary smell of rotting socks would hit you like a mallet as soon as you walked in the door; the offending aromas would penetrate every floor of the house. I did not eat Brussels sprouts for a very long time.

I promise that these are a far cry from any childhood horror. For those of you who still cannot eat (or bear the thought of) Brussels sprouts, you can make this salad with grilled zucchini or grilled corn. I won't hold it against you.

Serves 8 people

1 lb black rice (forbidden rice) — rinsed in cold water

3 cups water

1 1/2 lbs Brussels sprouts

Zest and juice of 2 lemons

3 tablespoons olive oil

Sea salt and black pepper

1 bunch chives — thinly sliced

1 bunch spring onions — ends trimmed and then stalks thinly sliced

1   Place the rice and water into a large saucepan placed over high heat. Add a pinch of salt and bring to a boil. As soon as the water boils, cover and reduce to a simmer. Cook for approximately 25 minutes or until the rice is tender and the water has been absorbed.

2   While the rice is cooking, prepare the Brussels sprouts. Bring a large saucepan of water to a boil. Pop the sprouts in the water and cook for 2 minutes. Drain the sprouts. When cool enough to handle, halve them. Place the cut sprouts into a bowl and drizzle with a little olive oil, a pinch of salt and some pepper. Toss to coat.

3   Heat a cast-iron grill pan. Add the Brussels sprouts and cook for 2–3 minutes on each side. They will still be a little crunchy. Once cooked, place the Brussels sprouts into a medium-sized salad bowl.

4   Add the cooked rice to the salad bowl with the Brussels sprouts. Pour the lemon juice and olive oil over the rice and sprouts mixture. Scatter the chives, spring onions and lemon zest on top, grind some black pepper over the salad and toss all the ingredients together well.

Red Quinoa with Blood Oranges, Pistachios, Herbs and Thyme-Encrusted Roasted Duck Legs

The first time I ate quinoa, I was intrigued by its grain-like texture and fine, slightly earthy taste. I wanted to find out more about this seed. It has been cultivated for more than 3,000 years in the Andes and was prized by the Inca. It grows in very inhospitable places and has to be harvested and threshed by hand. I appreciate every mouthful all the more, knowing the extraordinary efforts made by quinoa farmers to bring their crop to market.

It is a diverse seed that works well in salads; you can substitute it for couscous, for example, or in a tabbouleh for a more rustic dish. The earthiness pairs well with oranges and other fruit and with the richness of the duck. This dish is a favorite at home.

Serves 8 to 10 people

8 duck legs — trimmed of as much fat as possible

1 bunch fresh thyme

Coarse sea salt

Black pepper

2 cups red quinoa

4 cups water

5–6 shallots — peeled and thinly sliced

Zest of 4 blood oranges — the oranges also need to be peeled and the fruit chopped into very small pieces

1 tablespoon red wine vinegar or balsamic vinegar

1/2 cup pistachios

1 bunch chives — finely chopped

1/4 cup parsley — finely chopped

2 blood oranges — quartered

1 Preheat the oven to 350 degrees.

2 Place the duck legs on a sheet pan and carefully score the skin side of each leg, cutting slightly into the meat. Insert a sprig of thyme into each incision. Sprinkle a little sea salt and some black pepper over each leg. Place the pan in the center of the oven. Roast for 1 hour.

3 While the duck is cooking, prepare the quinoa. Place the quinoa in a saucepan with 4 cups of water and bring to a boil. Reduce to a simmer, cover and cook until the quinoa has absorbed all the water. You can also cook the quinoa in a rice cooker, using the same proportions.

4 While the quinoa is cooking, sauté the shallots with a little olive oil in a shallow, heavy-bottomed pan placed over medium heat. Cook until soft and translucent. Stir the orange zest into the shallots. Add a pinch of salt, some pepper and the vinegar. Set aside.

5 As soon as the quinoa is cooked, place it into a warmed serving dish and combine it with the cooked shallots, the orange pieces, pistachios and the chopped herbs. Toss to combine so that all the ingredients are well distributed throughout the quinoa.

6 To serve, spoon some of the quinoa onto the center of each dinner plate and top with a roasted duck leg. Squeeze the quartered blood oranges over each duck leg and serve at once.

Multi-Colored Quinoa Salad with Roasted Portobello Mushrooms

This salad combines the earthiness of mushrooms and quinoa. I like to make it when I come across some freshly picked mushrooms at the market, especially chanterelles or beautiful shiitake.

Serves 8 people

For the quinoa:

1 cup quinoa — carefully rinsed

2 cups water

Olive oil

1 medium-sized yellow onion — finely chopped

1 lb wild greens such as baby bok choy, dandelion greens, kale, or rapini — finely chopped

Sea salt and black pepper

$1/3$ cup blistered almonds — chopped

2 tablespoons chives — finely chopped

2 tablespoons parsley — finely chopped

2 tablespoons cilantro — finely chopped

For the mushrooms:

$1/4$ cup olive oil

1 tablespoon balsamic vinegar

1 teaspoon smoked salt such as Salish

1 tablespoon chives — finely chopped

8 large portobello mushrooms — stems removed, caps left intact

2 tablespoons butter

$1/2$ lb shiitake, chanterelles or other wild mushrooms — stems removed and thinly sliced

$1/4$ lb Stilton or other blue cheese such as Roquefort or Gorgonzola

1 Place the quinoa in a saucepan with the water and bring to a boil. Reduce to a simmer, cover and cook until the quinoa has absorbed all the water. You can also cook the quinoa in a rice cooker, using the same proportions.

2 Pour a little olive oil into a large skillet placed over medium heat. Add the onion and cook until soft and translucent. Add the greens and cook for 5-7 minutes. They should still be bright green. Add a little pinch of salt and some pepper and stir.

3 Once the greens are cooked, add the cooked quinoa, chopped almonds and all of the herbs. Combine well.

4 Preheat the oven to 400 degrees.

5 Combine the olive oil, vinegar, a good pinch of the smoked salt and chives in a bowl. Whisk together well. Add the portobello mushrooms to the bowl and carefully toss the mushrooms, taking care not to break them. Do this at least 30 minutes prior to baking them.

6 Place the mushrooms cap side down on a baking sheet and bake in the oven for 20 minutes.

7 While the portobello mushrooms are cooking, add the butter to a skillet placed over medium heat. Once the butter has melted, add the remaining wild mushrooms and sauté until just browned.

8 Remove the portobello mushrooms from the oven and spoon some of the sautéed mushrooms into the center of each portobello mushroom. Place some of the Stilton (or other blue cheese) on top, and return to the oven for 5-7 minutes more to allow the cheese to melt.

9 To serve, spoon some of the quinoa salad into the center of each dinner plate and place one of the large filled portobello mushrooms on top. Serve while hot.

Multi-Rice and Zucchini Salad

I like to think of this recipe as a template to be built upon and modified as the seasons evolve. Its flavor can vary depending on the types of rice and squash used. That is part of its charm. You can for example, substitute jasmine rice for the basmati, or add wild rice to the mix. In the autumn and winter, I like to replace summer zucchini with roasted acorn or butternut squash in this salad, which makes a wonderful side dish for any large gathering such as Thanksgiving. I always enjoy creating new versions, and I hope you do too!

Serves 8 people

For the salad:

1 $1/2$ cups assorted rice (mix of black, wild, red) — well rinsed

3 cups water

$1/2$ cup basmati rice — well rinsed

$3/4$ cup water

Salt

Olive oil

1 lb round or patty pan squash or small zucchini — sliced

1 large red onion or 2 torpedo onions — peeled and diced

1 tablespoon za'atar

Black pepper

$1/4$ cup finely chopped chives

$1/4$ cup finely chopped parsley

$1/4$ cup golden raisins

$1/4$ cup salted pistachios

Zest and juice of 1 lemon

For the vinaigrette:

$1/4$ cup olive oil

Zest and juice of 1 lemon

1 tablespoon white wine vinegar or Champagne vinegar

Large pinch of coarse sea salt

8–10 grinds of black pepper

1 Pre-heat the oven to 375 degrees.

2 Place the assorted rice and 3 cups water in a large saucepan with a pinch of salt. Bring to a boil. Reduce heat to low. Cover and cook for 25–30 minutes, or until rice is tender and the water has been absorbed.

3 Place the basmati rice and $3/4$ cup water in a small saucepan with a pinch of salt. Bring to a boil. Reduce heat to low. Cover and cook for 20–25 minutes, or until rice is tender and the water has been absorbed.

4 Pour a little olive oil into a large baking dish or onto a baking sheet. Add the zucchini and onions. Shake the pan back and forth to coat. Sprinkle the za'atar, a good pinch of salt and 7–8 grinds of black pepper over the vegetables. Roast in oven for 40–45 minutes. The zucchini should be golden brown.

5 In a medium mixing bowl, whisk together all the vinaigrette ingredients to form an emulsion. Add all the cooked rice, roasted vegetables, and all the remaining salad ingredients, and gently toss to mix well. Serve on a large platter or in a shallow dish.

FAVA BEANS, HARICOTS VERTS & PEAS

Haricots Verts Salad

—

PB Salad

—

Snap Pea, Mint
and White Peach
Salad with Pistachio
Vinaigrette

—

Watercress and
Spring Pea Salad

—

Cherry, Pea and Fava
Bean Salad

Haricots Verts Salad

This is another one of those classic French salads. Every time my grandmother or my mother made a roasted leg of lamb, she would serve this alongside. I love the slight bite of the shallots and mustard vinaigrette with the dainty haricots verts.

Serves 8 people

2 lbs haricots verts —
   ends trimmed

2 shallots — peeled and
   finely chopped

Sea salt and black pepper

1 tablespoon Dijon mustard

4 tablespoons olive oil

1 tablespoon white wine
   vinegar or tarragon
   vinegar

I bunch chives —
   finely chopped

1 Place the haricots verts in a steamer and cook for 5–7 minutes. The haricots verts should still be bright green and al dente. As soon as they are cooked, remove them from the steamer and rinse under cold water. Drain.

2 Place the shallots in a small bowl with a good pinch of salt and some pepper. Stir the shallots and the salt and leave for 5 minutes before making the vinaigrette. (This helps soften the flavor of the shallots.)

3 Combine the mustard, olive oil and vinegar in a salad bowl and whisk together to create an emulsion. Add the shallots, the cooked haricots verts and the chives, and toss well to combine.

PB Salad

Walking through the Santa Barbara Farmers Market on an early Saturday morning, I came across a bunch of edible nasturtiums. They ranged in color from sunflower yellow to pumpkin orange and proved to be irresistible. Lying in the basket next to them were some pea tendrils. If you have never had them, please try to find some. They taste absolutely fresh and delicious when lightly sautéed in a little olive oil with a squeeze of lemon juice. They are also a versatile addition to many salads.

I had a couple of bunches of golden beets in my basket and imagined all these colorful ingredients coming together in a salad bowl. When I spied the fava beans, my salad was complete — in my mind that is.

My lovely Mum was coming over for lunch later that day, and this is the salad I made for her. The PB stands for peas and beets.

Serves 8 people

Olive oil

6 medium-sized golden beets — peeled and thinly sliced on a mandolin

1 teaspoon white wine vinegar or pear Champagne vinegar

1 large red onion — peeled, quartered and thinly sliced

1 lb snap peas — thinly sliced on a bias

1 lb fava beans — shelled (you will need to remove the bean from the pod and then the outer shell of the fava bean — it's easier if you blanch them first for 2 minutes)

1 large bunch pea tendrils — roughly chopped

3 tablespoons orange juice (blood orange if possible)

3 tablespoons olive oil

1 tablespoon fig balsamic vinegar

Sea salt and black pepper

1 small bunch edible nasturtiums — stems removed

1 Pour a little olive oil into a large skillet placed over medium heat. Place the beet slices in the pan so that they barely overlap. (You will probably have to do this in 2 or 3 batches.) Drizzle a little of the white wine vinegar over the top and cook for 3–4 minutes, turning the beets once or twice. The beets should be just cooked through. Remove the pan from the heat, leaving the beets in the pan, covered for 3–4 minutes.

2 Pour a little olive oil into a large pan placed over medium-high heat. Add the sliced onions and cook for 5–6 minutes so that they are soft but not browned. Scatter the snap peas over the onions, stir and cook for 2 minutes. Toss in the pea tendrils and fava beans and cook, stirring frequently, for another minute or so. The tendrils will just start to wilt. As soon as they do, spoon all of this mixture into a salad bowl.

3 Combine the orange juice, fig balsamic vinegar and olive oil in a small bowl and whisk together well. Sprinkle in a good pinch of salt and some pepper and whisk once more to form a smooth emulsion.

4 Add the cooked beets to the salad bowl and drizzle with the vinaigrette. Toss to combine. Divide the salad between the salad plates and place the nasturtium flowers on top of each salad.

Snap Pea, Mint and White Peach Salad with Pistachio Vinaigrette

I often slice fruits and vegetables in different ways, experimenting with shapes and arrangements when plating dishes. Some vegetables are not that exciting when cut open, eggplant for example, but others are divine, and there is something exquisitely simple and beautiful about peas lying exposed in their pods. This is a salad that celebrates summer, when snap peas are bursting with flavor, grassy-sweet and tender.

Serves 8 people

For the salad:

Olive oil

1 1/2 lbs snap peas — ends trimmed, then pods cut in half on a bias

Salt

Black pepper

6 white peaches — halved, pitted and thinly sliced

1/2 cup mint leaves

1/2 cup assorted basil leaves (Thai, lemon, Italian)

Zest of 1 lemon

For the vinaigrette:

1/3 cup pistachios

1/4 cup olive oil

1 tablespoon red wine vinegar or pear Champagne vinegar

1 teaspoon finely chopped chives

Salt

Black pepper

1 Pour a drizzle of olive oil into a large skillet placed over medium-high heat. Once the oil is hot, add the snap peas, a good pinch of salt and 4–5 grinds of pepper, and sauté for 1–2 minutes. Remove the pan from the heat. Transfer the snap peas to a large platter. Add the peach slices to the snap peas and arrange them together in an attractive manner. Scatter the mint and basil leaves over the top.

2 In a small skillet, toast the pistachios over medium heat, just until fragrant (less than 2 minutes), being careful not to burn them. Remove the skillet from the heat and add the olive oil, vinegar, chives, a good pinch of salt and 5–6 grinds of black pepper to the pan. Whisk together to form an emulsion. Pour the warm vinaigrette over the salad, then dot with the lemon zest.

Watercress and Spring Pea Salad

One of my cousins in France told me she thought it was odd that I put fruit in my salads. I asked her to taste the peach and tomato salad I made for her, and she has been a convert ever since. This salad has blueberries and mint, and a little zing in it. It's very refreshing!

Serves 8 people

Zest and juice of 1 lemon

3 tablespoons olive oil

Sea salt and black pepper

1 lb fava beans — shelled (you will need to remove the beans from the pods, and then the outer shell of the fava bean — it's easier if you blanch them first for 2 minutes)

1 lb English peas — shelled

2 bunches watercress leaves

2 good handfuls mint leaves — try to use just small leaves

1/2 bunch cilantro leaves

2 baskets blueberries

4 oz feta cheese — crumbled

1 Combine the olive oil with the lemon zest and juice, a pinch of salt and 4–5 grinds of black pepper in the bottom of a salad bowl. Whisk together briskly. Place salad utensils over the vinaigrette.

2 Pour a little olive oil (really just a touch) into a medium-sized skillet placed over medium heat. Add the peas and fava beans to the skillet and cook for no more than 2–3 minutes. Do not overcook them. Spoon the cooked peas and beans into the salad bowl, on top of the utensils. Place all the remaining ingredients in the bowl on top of the peas and fava beans.

3 When you are ready to serve the salad, toss gently so that everything is well combined.

Cherry, Pea and Fava Bean Salad

The fava bean and cherry seasons overlap for about four weeks, which doesn't give you much time to make this salad. You see the cherries but not the fava beans, then the beans but not the cherries. However, when you do get both of them together, they are magical. This salad is the essence of spring.

Serves 8 people

Olive oil

4 shallots — peeled
    and sliced

1/2 lb English peas — shelled

1/2 lb snap peas — sliced
    on a bias

1 lb fava beans — shelled
    (you will need to remove
    the beans from the pods,
    and then the outer shell
    of the fava bean — it's
    easier if you blanch them
    first for 2 minutes)

Sea salt and black pepper

1 lb cherries — pitted
    and halved

Zest and juice of 1 lemon

1/2 cup basil leaves

1/2 cup mint leaves

1   Pour a little olive oil into a skillet placed over medium heat. Add the shallots and cook for 5 minutes. Add the peas, snap peas and fava beans, a pinch of salt and some pepper and cook for 3 minutes. Remove from the heat and set aside.

2   Pour 3 tablespoons olive oil into the bottom of a salad bowl and then whisk in the lemon zest and juice, a pinch of salt and some black pepper. Place salad utensils over the vinaigrette and then add the cherries to the bowl. Place the mint and basil leaves on top of the cherries and add the cooked peas and fava beans mixture to the bowl.

3   When you are ready to serve the salad, toss the ingredients well. You can make a different version using chives and cilantro leaves instead of the basil leaves.

LENTILS, POTATOES & ROASTED VEGETABLES

Lentils du Puy Salad
with Spiced Greek
Yogurt

—

Black Lentils with
Roasted Eggplant and
Tomatoes

—

Warm Dandelion
and Watercress
Salad with Roasted
Root Vegetables,
Bacon and Herbs

—

Roasted Kale and
Sweet Potato Salad

—

Roasted Cauliflower
and Chive Salad with
Yogurt-Herb Sauce

—

Smashed Herbed
Potatoes

Lentils du Puy Salad with Spiced Greek Yogurt

The French make a great deal of fuss about these lentils and just how good they are. I am a complete fan to the point where I don't really want to make any lentil dish without them. You may think that a lentil is a lentil is a lentil, but when it comes to these little slate green gems, that is not true. These are the *nec plus ultra* of lentils. That said, there's a recipe for black lentils on the next page, and actually they're pretty good, too — but I have to give the edge to these.

One of the best lentil salads I have ever had was in a little café in St. Tropez, which, unfortunately, no longer exists in its original incarnation. The lady who ran the restaurant knew her lentils. The salad was simple, served with a vinaigrette and some herbs. The lentils weren't goopy or mushy. You tasted each one. Perfect. My lentil salads aspire to that one.

Serves 8 people

2 cups Lentils du Puy
(French lentils — they are
small and dark green)

4 cups boiling water

3 bay leaves

Olive oil

2 medium red onions —
peeled and finely diced

2 cloves garlic — peeled and
minced

2 teaspoons Ras al Hanout

1 teaspoon curry powder

1 lb baby kale —
finely chopped

2 cups Greek yogurt

1/2 bunch Italian parsley
leaves

1/2 bunch chives —
finely chopped

Juice and zest of 1 lemon

Sea salt and black pepper

1 Place the lentils and bay leaves in a large saucepan filled with boiling water and cook for 20–30 minutes. They should be al dente. Drain and set aside.

2 Pour a little olive oil into a medium-sized skillet placed over medium-low heat. Add the onions, garlic, the Ras al Hanout and curry powder. Cook for 8–10 minutes until the onions are very soft and translucent. Add the chopped kale and cook until the kale has wilted, about 4–5 minutes. Set aside to cool.

3 Place the yogurt in a large salad bowl. Add the cooked onion-kale mixture and the herbs. Toss to coat well. Add the lentils, lemon juice, lemon zest, a good pinch of salt and some black pepper and toss again to combine.

Black Lentils with Roasted Eggplant and Tomatoes

Given how I feel about Lentils du Puy (see previous recipe) I was a little skeptical the first time I tried black lentils. I am always happy to be proved wrong when it comes to anything culinary, and these lentils were delicious. I love their earthy, rich flavor which works particularly well when combined with roasted vegetables and caramelized tomatoes.

This is a hearty dish that can be the centerpiece of a plant-based dinner, or served as a side dish with roast chicken or grilled fish.

Serves 8 people

1 1/2 lbs eggplant — cut into 1/2-inch cubes

Olive oil

Sea salt

Black pepper

1 tablespoon fresh thyme leaves

Leaves from 6-7 sprigs oregano

3/4 lb red cherry tomatoes

2 cups black lentils — rinsed well

8 cups hot water

1/4 lb baby spinach leaves

Juice and zest of 2 lemons

1 cup Greek yogurt

1/4 cup finely chopped chives

1 Preheat the oven to 350 degrees.

2 Place the eggplant on a baking sheet, ensuring the pieces are not overcrowded. Drizzle lightly with olive oil. Add a good pinch of sea salt and 10-12 grinds of black pepper. Scatter the thyme and oregano over the top. Using your hands, toss to mix well. Roast the eggplant for 1 hour, turning with a spatula once or twice. They should be completely soft and golden brown.

3 Place the cherry tomatoes in an ovenproof dish that is just large enough to hold them. Drizzle with some olive oil. Add a pinch of salt and some black pepper. Roast for 25-30 minutes in the same oven as the eggplant. They will start to render juice and should get a little wrinkled.

4 Place the lentils and hot water into a large saucepan. Cover and simmer gently until the lentils are cooked, approximately 20 minutes. Taste them. They should be tender, but not overly so. Be sure NOT to overcook the lentils or they will be mushy. Drain the lentils of any remaining liquid, and place in a large bowl. Immediately stir in spinach leaves, 1/4 cup of olive oil, the juice and zest of 1 lemon, a large pinch of sea salt and 10-12 grinds of black pepper. The heat from the lentils will slightly wilt the spinach leaves.

5 Add the roasted eggplant and tomatoes to the bowl. Combine gently so that the tomatoes are not squished.

6 In a small bowl, stir together yogurt, chives and the juice and zest of the remaining lemon. Dot the surface of the salad with dollops of the yogurt sauce.

Warm Dandelion and Watercress Salad with Roasted Root Vegetables, Bacon and Herbs

This salad came about as a result of a *Tour de Frigidaire,* or TDF as my friend Michele would say. It's a great expression that means making something out of all the bits that are left in your fridge. The first time I made this, there were three of us having an impromptu lunch. Here's the recipe for eight. Feel free to add other bits and pieces (goat cheese or feta would be great, for example) from your own *frigidaire*!

Serves 8 people

Olive oil

1 lb multi-colored carrots — peeled and cut into 2-inch pieces

1 large parsnip — peeled and chopped into long strips

2 lbs beets — golden, ruby or red — peeled and cut into quarters

4 slices of bacon — cut crosswise into thin strips

2 sprigs of fresh rosemary leaves

Sea salt and black pepper

1 tablespoon fig balsamic vinegar

8 oz dandelion greens — cleaned and roughly chopped

8 oz watercress — cleaned and roughly chopped

1/2 bunch dill — finely chopped

1/2 bunch parsley — finely chopped

1/2 bunch basil leaves — rolled up and thinly sliced

1 Preheat the oven to 350 degrees.

2 Pour a little olive oil onto a baking sheet and add the carrots, parsnips, beets, bacon strips, fresh rosemary and some salt and pepper. Toss to coat well. Roast in the oven for 45 minutes until tender. Stir the vegetables once or twice while they are cooking.

3 Pour a 1/4 cup olive oil into a salad bowl. Whisk in the fig balsamic vinegar, add a pinch of salt and some pepper. Place salad utensils over the vinaigrette. Place the dandelion and watercress on top of the utensils.

4 When you are ready to serve the salad, add all the roasted vegetables to the salad bowl and all of the remaining chopped herbs. Toss until well combined.

Roasted Kale and Sweet Potato Salad

My lovely Mum adores sweet potatoes. She would bring me some from the market, a not so subtle hint, I believe, that I should try to incorporate more of them into my food. I think I had resisted cooking with them because I didn't like the fact that they were almost too sweet. The more I have experimented, however, the more versatile I realize they are. When roasted for example, they pair sublimely with earthy-flavored ingredients, such as lentils, grilled mushrooms, Brussels sprouts, or as in this case, with slightly crispy kale. The salad, with its creamy avocado vinaigrette and crunchy pistachios, is an amalgam of savory and sweet. Thank you, Mum, for always encouraging me to push my boundaries.

Serves 8 people

For the salad:

1 lb curly kale — rinsed (but not dried), de-stemmed and chopped into 1-inch wide strips

Olive oil

Sea salt

Black pepper

2 large sweet potatoes — peeled, halved lengthwise, then cut into $1/4$-inch thick slices

2 teaspoons Herbes de Poisson (or an equal mixture of fennel seeds, coriander seeds and brown mustard seeds)

$1/3$ cup roughly chopped pistachios

For the vinaigrette:

$1/4$ cup olive oil

1 tablespoon white wine vinegar — or Champagne vinegar

1 avocado — peeled and the meat scooped out

Juice of 1 lemon

Sea salt

Black pepper

1 Preheat the oven to 350 degrees.

2 Place the kale onto a large rimmed sheet pan or into a shallow baking dish. Drizzle with olive oil and sprinkle with 2–3 pinches of salt and 5–6 grinds of pepper. Roast in the center of the oven for 8 minutes. Place the lightly cooked kale into a large salad bowl.

3 Using the same pan, lay the sweet potato slices out in a single layer. Use a second sheet pan, if they appear overcrowded. Drizzle with a little olive oil and sprinkle the Herbes de Poisson over the top. Roast for 20–25 minutes, turning the potatoes over once. They should be fork tender and lightly browned. Place the roasted sweet potato slices on top of the kale.

4 To make the vinaigrette, pour the olive oil into a small bowl and whisk in the vinegar. Add the avocado meat and mash together with a fork. Add the lemon juice, a good pinch of salt and 8–10 grinds of pepper, and whisk with the fork so that all the ingredients form a homogenous, though slightly chunky, vinaigrette. Spoon the vinaigrette and sprinkle the pistachios over the salad. Serve warm.

Roasted Cauliflower and Chive Salad with Yogurt-Herb Sauce

Whilst on a book tour in Northern California last year, I once again stayed with my good friends Kristen and Allen in their lovely home in the Berkeley Hills. I made dinner one night, (this has become a tradition) to thank them for their always generous hospitality. I went shopping in the local, iconic, organic food emporium, Berkeley Bowl, and had gone slightly bonkers, seduced by so many ingredients. I made a multitude of dishes, including this one which I photographed on their dining room table as the sun set over San Francisco Bay. Merci mes amis!

Serves 8 people

For the salad:

1 head cauliflower — broken into small florets

4 green onions — root ends removed, finely chopped

$1/4$ cup finely chopped chives

Olive oil

Sea salt

Black pepper

For the yogurt-herb sauce:

1 cup Greek yogurt

$1/4$ cup finely chopped chives

$1/4$ cup finely chopped parsley

2 tablespoons finely chopped dill

3 tablespoons olive oil

Zest and juice of 1 lemon

Large pinch of sea salt

6–8 grinds of black pepper

1 Preheat the oven to 375 degrees.

2 Place the cauliflower florets, chopped green onions and chives onto a baking sheet or into a shallow roasting pan. Drizzle with a little olive oil and shake the pan a few times to coat well. Sprinkle with a couple of pinches of salt and 6–8 grinds of pepper. Roast for 20–25 minutes until the florets are just starting to brown and they are just knife tender. Place the vegetables in a salad bowl.

3 In a small bowl, combine all the yogurt sauce ingredients. Serve alongside the cauliflower.

Smashed Herbed Potatoes

I had just seen a video of an exuberant Jamie Oliver waxing lyrical about the joys of roast spuds, when, later that morning, I spied some of my favorite tubers — fingerling potatoes — at the farmers' market. Of course, I couldn't get the idea of roasting potatoes out of my head, so once home, I made these for lunch, along with a green salad and some burrata. My son and I demolished the entire dish. As Jamie would say, it was just "lovely jubbly!"

Serves 8 people

1 1/2 lbs baby potatoes or fingerling potatoes

Olive oil

Salt

Black pepper

1/2 cup finely chopped parsley

1 tablespoon finely chopped chives

1 tablespoon finely chopped tarragon

1 teaspoon chopped fresh thyme leaves

1 Preheat the oven to 400 degrees.

2 Bring a large saucepan of water to a boil. Add the potatoes and a pinch of salt. Cook until potatoes are just barely tender, about 8–10 minutes depending on their size. Drain and place the potatoes on a rimmed sheet pan.

3 Using a fork or the back of a spoon, gently squash the potatoes so that the skin splits, but the potatoes are not completely exploded. Drizzle about 4 tablespoons of olive oil over the potatoes. Sprinkle a generous pinch of salt and 10–12 grinds of pepper over the top. Shake the pan once or twice to coat well. Roast for 30 minutes until the potatoes are golden and slightly crispy. Add the herbs to the pan and toss to mix well. Return the pan to the oven and roast for another 5 minutes. Serve hot.

MUSHROOMS

Warm Mushroom
and White
Asparagus Salad

—

Wild Mushroom
and Pea Salad

—

Baby Arugula, Wild
Mushroom and Goat
Cheese Salad

—

Salade des Cousinades

—

Wild Mushroom
Crostini Salad

Warm Mushroom and White Asparagus Salad

This salad contains two of my favorite ingredients — white asparagus and wild mushrooms. If the wild mushrooms happen to be chanterelles, even better. Honestly, there are few things that are more mouth watering than the aroma of sizzling butter in a pan with sliced mushrooms cooking in it. Sometimes I'll cook a few mushrooms to add to a green salad or put on some toast with a piece of goat cheese. I love their earthy flavors. White asparagus have a herbaceous quality to them. They balance the rustic qualities of the mushrooms in this salad. It's a dish I look forward to every spring as we emerge from winter.

Serves 8 people

For the salad:

2 lbs white asparagus — carefully peeled, tips cut off, and stems cut on a bias in 1-inch pieces

Olive oil

2 shallots — peeled and finely sliced

1 tablespoon butter

1 1/2 lbs assorted wild mushrooms — cleaned and sliced

1 bunch chives — finely chopped

For the vinaigrette:

1 teaspoon Dijon mustard

3 tablespoons olive oil

1 tablespoon vinegar

Sea salt and black pepper

1 Place the asparagus in a steamer or in a large pan of lightly salted boiling water and cook for 6–7 minutes until just al dente. Remove, drain and set aside.

2 While the asparagus are cooking, pour a little olive oil into a large skillet placed over medium-high heat. Add the shallots and cook until just golden, about 3 minutes. Add a tablespoon of butter and then the sliced mushrooms. Cook until golden brown. Sprinkle in the chives. Cook for 1 minute more and then set aside.

3 For the vinaigrette, combine the mustard, olive oil and vinegar in a large salad bowl and whisk until you have an emulsion. Add in a pinch of salt and some black pepper. Place serving utensils over the vinaigrette and then add the asparagus and mushrooms to the bowl, on top of the utensils. When you are ready to serve, toss the salad carefully and divide between eight plates.

Wild Mushroom and Pea Salad

This is a fresh, crunchy salad with lots of tasty, golden mushrooms in it. You can use any blue cheese — I like to use a creamy Stilton — and any combination of mushrooms. If you don't like blue cheese, use feta. Try to serve this whilst the ingredients are still warm, as the cheese melts slightly and makes it even more delectable.

Serves 8 people

For the salad:

1 tablespoon butter

1 lb assorted wild mushrooms — cleaned and sliced

Olive oil

1 lb English peas, snap peas (cut on a bias), green peas

For the vinaigrette:

1/4 cup olive oil

1 tablespoon pear Champagne vinegar

Sea salt and black pepper

2 tablespoons chives — finely chopped

1 tablespoon blue cheese

1 Place the butter in a large pan over medium-high heat and add the sliced mushrooms. Cook until just browned. Remove the mushrooms from the pan before they start to render any water. Set aside on a plate.

2 Return the pan to the heat and add a little olive oil. Add all the peas and cook for 3–4 minutes so that they are cooked through but still somewhat firm.

3 In a large salad bowl, whisk together the olive oil and vinegar. Stir in some salt and pepper and all the chives. Place serving utensils over the vinaigrette and add the blue cheese, wild mushrooms and peas on top. When you are ready to serve the salad, toss to combine the ingredients well.

Baby Arugula, Wild Mushroom and Goat Cheese Salad

Robert Dautch, or BD, as he is known to everyone, has been farming for more than four decades in the Ojai Valley. I have heard him described as an "organic alchemist" and, having cooked with his exquisite array of herbs, greens, edible flowers and vegetables for many of those years, I can attest that he and his hard-working crew are masters of their craft. He is also a fountain of knowledge, and it was he, when he saw that I held a bunch of his Japanese globe turnips in my hand one market day, who said "you know those are great eaten raw, Pascale." I had not, up to that point, tried raw turnips, but dutifully went home and tried one. The texture and flavor were a revelation: sweet, delicate, with a hint of a mild radish on the palate, and the crunch of an Asian pear. They are terrific in salads. In this recipe they add a delicate yet crunchy contrast to the warmth of the sautéed mushrooms, the creaminess of the goat cheese and the pepperiness of the arugula.

Serves 8 people

For the vinaigrette:

1 tablespoon walnut mustard

1/4 cup extra virgin olive oil

1 tablespoon Champagne or white wine vinegar

For the salad:

8 oz baby arugula

2 oz sprouted mung beans

4-5 baby Japanese globe turnips — washed (and peeled if necessary), then thinly sliced

2 tablespoons finely chopped chives

3 oz goat cheese

2 tablespoons olive oil

2 tablespoons butter

1 1/2 lbs assorted mushrooms, including cremini, trumpet, shitake — sliced

Sea salt

Black pepper

1 In a large salad bowl, whisk together the vinaigrette ingredients to form a thick emulsion. Place salad utensils over the vinaigrette.

2 Place the arugula, mung beans, sliced turnips, chives and goat cheese on top of the utensils.

3 Pour the olive oil into a large skillet over medium heat. When the oil is just sizzling, add the butter and melt until foaming. Add the mushrooms, a good pinch of salt and 8-10 grinds of pepper. Sauté, stirring frequently, until golden brown, about 5-6 minutes. Add the mushrooms to the salad. Toss to combine well. Serve while the mushrooms are still warm.

Salade des Cousinades

Every few years, my family in France gets together for an event we call *Les Cousinades*, literally "the cousins' get-together." Each event is organized by one cousin, usually in an area known for very good food. We are a family that is, for the most part, somewhat obsessed with anything culinary. On one of these family pilgrimages, 55 of us (yes, all related to each other) took over a restaurant in Sarlat in the Périgord-Dordogne region, a town known for its golden-colored architecture and all things related to duck and cèpes (porcini). Lunch began with a *Salade aux Cèpes.* The mushrooms and accompanying potatoes had been sautéed in duck fat. It was very good. This is my version of that salad, a tribute to my cousins.

Serves 8 people

For the vinaigrette:

2 tablespoons olive oil

1 tablespoon truffle oil

1 tablespoon red wine
vinegar or Jerez vinegar

Large pinch of sea salt

8–10 grinds of black pepper

For the salad:

1/2 lb fresh or 4 oz dried
porcini mushrooms

1 1/2 lbs wild mushrooms —
finely sliced

8 oz small new potatoes or
fingerling potatoes

2 tablespoons duck fat

2 tablespoons butter

4 oz mache salad greens

1 bunch chives —
finely chopped

Sea salt and black pepper

1 Combine all of the vinaigrette ingredients in the bottom of a large salad bowl and whisk together until you have a smooth vinaigrette. If you like the vinaigrette to be a little sweeter, add a little more of the vinegar. Place the serving utensils over the vinaigrette.

2 Soak the dried porcini mushrooms in a small bowl of boiling hot water, or vegetable stock, for 20 minutes. (Omit this step if using fresh mushrooms.) Drain the mushrooms.

3 While the mushrooms are soaking, cook the potatoes in a large saucepan of boiling salted water for about 10–15 minutes. Drain, then slice thinly.

4 Pour a little duck fat into a large sauté pan and sauté the sliced potatoes until golden brown on both sides. Spoon the cooked potatoes into the salad bowl.

5 Add the butter to the same sauté pan, and cook the mushrooms (each variety separately). They will only need a few minutes each. Add them to the salad bowl.

6 Place the mache and chives on top of the potatoes and mushrooms. Sprinkle with a large pinch of salt and 8–10 grinds of pepper. Toss the salad when you are ready to serve.

Wild Mushroom Crostini Salad

My long-time friends Frederic and Fatos owned one of my favorite restaurants in Santa Barbara. The setting was hip and romantic, a mix of jazz bands played on a weekly basis, serenading guests to Django Reinhardt riffs and bluesy vibes. It was the place where you'd pop in for a savory nibble at the bar, or lounge over a long Mediterranean-styled meal on the terrace. It was my *bistro du coin*. One of my favorite items on the appetizer menu was a deceptively named dish, a single *Mushroom Toast*. The toast in question was piled high with a giant mound of shaved mushrooms that had been mixed with truffles and some grated cheese. It was so succulently decadent. This salad is a little tribute to that dish, and the lovely times spent with everyone at The Little Door.

Serves 8 people

For the salad:

7 oz mixed salad greens

For the vinaigrette:

1 tablespoon Dijon mustard

3 tablespoons olive oil

1 tablespoon white wine vinegar or Champagne vinegar

Pinch of coarse sea salt

8–10 grinds of black pepper

For the crostini:

2 oz butter

Olive oil

2 lbs wild mushrooms — cleaned and thinly sliced

2 tablespoons finely chopped chives

3 tablespoons crème fraiche

3 oz grated Manchego or Gruyere cheese

16 thin slices baguette — toasted

1 Cover a large platter or shallow bowl with the salad greens.

2 In a small bowl, whisk together the vinaigrette ingredients to form an emulsion. Set aside.

3 In a large skillet placed over medium heat, melt the butter with 1 tablespoon olive oil until the butter foams. Add the sliced mushrooms and cook until golden brown, about 3–4 minutes, stirring frequently. Depending on the size of your skillet, you may have to do this in batches, as you do not want to overcrowd the mushrooms in the pan. If necessary, add a little more olive oil to the second batch if the mushrooms seem too dry.

4 Place the cooked mushrooms, chives, crème fraiche and two-thirds of the cheese into a medium-sized mixing bowl. Stir to combine. Spoon the mixture onto the toasted baguette slices to make the crostini.

5 Pour the vinaigrette over the salad greens. Place the prepared crostini on top of the greens and top with the remaining grated cheese. Serve while the crostini are still warm.

NECTARINES, PEACHES & PLUMS

Nectarine, Buffalo Mozzarella and Fennel Salad

—

Plum and Watercress Salad

—

Grilled Peach and Tomato Salad with Peach Bellini Vinaigrette

—

Mache, Mint and Pluot Salad

—

White Nectarine Carpaccio with a Microgreen Salad

—

Peach, Melon and Prosciutto Salad

—

Arugula, Basil and Cilantro Salad with Pistachio Dukkah-Crusted Pluots

Nectarine, Buffalo Mozzarella and Fennel Salad

Many years ago on a trip to Italy, I had the ubiquitous tomato and mozzarella salad. I was going to order something else, but the waiter insisted that I have the salad as the mozzarella had just arrived and was fresh. I realized, in hindsight, that I had no clue what he meant by "fresh." He meant made-in-the-last-12-hours fresh. The plate arrived with some sliced tomatoes and a whole mozzarella in the middle. A bottle of olive oil was placed on the table. There was also some salt and pepper — nothing else. This did not look promising. Then I took a bite. The waiter had been watching me. I looked at him in amazement. He just nodded and smiled. I have never — to this day — tasted mozzarella like that. It was rich, creamy and soft, yet just firm enough to hold together. This was mozzarella perfection.

Don't get me wrong, I have found good mozzarella since then, and when I do, I like to tear it into small pieces and add it to all sorts of salads. This is one of them.

Serves 8 people

3 tablespoons olive oil

1 tablespoon Champagne vinegar

Pinch of sea salt

5–6 grinds of black pepper

4–6 medium-sized ripe nectarines — pitted and sliced

1 lb fresh buffalo mozzarella — gently torn into bite-sized pieces

1 fennel bulb — cut in half and then thinly sliced

2 white endives — root end trimmed and leaves separated

1/2 bunch chives — finely chopped

1/2 bunch dill — finely chopped

1 In a medium-sized, shallow salad bowl, whisk together the olive oil, vinegar, salt and pepper. Place salad utensils over the vinaigrette.

2 Place all the remaining ingredients on top of the salad utensils. When you are ready to serve the salad, remove the utensils and toss all the ingredients together gently.

Plum and Watercress Salad

I have a prolific plum tree in my garden. This year we had another bumper crop, and after two huge batches of jam, I still had plums all over the kitchen. We used them in everything — with roasted chicken, clafoutis, plum cake and salads. This was one of the favorites from the summer.

Serves 8 people

1/4 cup olive oil

1/2 bunch cilantro — chopped

1/2 bunch basil — chopped

Juice and zest of 1 lemon

Juice and zest of 1 lime

Sea salt

Black pepper

16 plums — pitted and thinly sliced

8 oz watercress

2 oz mixed nuts (pistachios, macadamias, walnuts, almonds) — chopped and then dry roasted in a pan for 2 minutes

2 oz feta cheese — crumbled

1 Place the olive oil, cilantro, basil, lemon zest and juice, lime zest and juice, a pinch of salt and 3–4 twists of pepper in a blender. Purée until smooth.

2 Pour the herb vinaigrette into the bottom of a large salad bowl and then place serving utensils on top of the vinaigrette.

3 Place the watercress and plum slices on top of the serving utensils.

4 When you are ready to serve the salad, toss to combine well. Divide the salad equally between the plates and then sprinkle the chopped nuts and the feta over the top of each salad.

Grilled Peach and Tomato Salad with Peach Bellini Vinaigrette

It was during a conversation with a friend of mine about the pleasures of Venice — getting lost along the lesser known canals, finding minute squares with jewel box chapels, the pastel shades of the palazzo, the local food, and of course, Peach Bellini — that the idea for this vinaigrette popped into my head. It helped that this conversation took place in the middle of my local farmers' market, and that we had just tasted a sublime peach. I bought some of course, and later that night, grilled a few peaches for a salad I was making. The grilling intensified the flavors of the peaches, caramelizing the juices a little as they cooked, and paired beautifully with the acidity in the tomatoes. I had put one peach aside to make a purée for the vinaigrette and was delighted with the result. We toasted Giuseppe Cipriani that evening, in honor of his frothy cocktail, and for inspiring what has become one of my new favorite summer salads.

Serves 8 people

For the vinaigrette:

1/4 cup olive oil

Juice and zest of 1 lemon

1 ripe peach

1 tablespoon Champagne vinegar

Pinch of coarse salt

10 grinds of black pepper

For the salad:

2 lbs large heirloom tomatoes — approximately the same size as the peaches, halved and cut into wedges

4–6 large peaches — halved, pitted and cut into wedges

2 tablespoons basil olive oil

Sea salt

Black pepper

1/2 cup packed mint leaves

1/4 cup Thai basil leaves

1 tablespoon pistachios

1 Place all the vinaigrette ingredients in a blender or food processor, and pulse until you have a smooth, homogenous vinaigrette. Keep refrigerated until ready to use.

2 Place the tomatoes into a large salad bowl or a large shallow platter.

3 Heat a griddle pan over a medium-hot flame on the stove.

4 Place the peaches into a medium-sized bowl. Pour the olive oil over the slices. Toss gently so that the peaches are coated. Sprinkle a little salt and pepper over the peaches. Place the peaches on the griddle and cook for 90 seconds. Carefully turn the peaches over and cook for 60 seconds on the other side. The peaches should have char marks on them.

5 Carefully remove the peaches from the griddle and add them to the tomatoes. Scatter the mint, basil leaves and pistachios over the fruit.

6 Drizzle the Peach Bellini vinaigrette over the salad, toss carefully so as not to break the fruit; serve immediately.

Mache, Mint and Pluot Salad

I am a fairly recent convert to pluots. I used to regard them as some sort of weird hybrid thing. I preferred plums to be plums and apricots, well, apricots. It was only when a local farmer urged me to overcome my reticence and actually try one that I realized the error of my ways. The fruit was delicious — a true reflection of its parental roots. When cut open, pluots reveal an array of jewel-toned colors and have marvelous names such as Dapple Dandy, Flavor Grenade and Raspberry Jewel. They make incredible jams. They also add sweet floral notes to salads.

Serves 8 people

For the vinaigrette:

Juice of 2 large lemons
   (or 3 small ones)

Large pinch of coarse
   sea salt

1/2 tablespoon honey

1/3 cup olive oil

8–10 grinds of black pepper

For the salad:

2 oz pine nuts

1/2 teaspoon fennel seeds

1/2 teaspoon mustard seeds

1/2 teaspoon coriander seeds

8 oz mache (lamb's lettuce)

8–10 pluots (use different
   varieties) — sliced

2 handfuls golden raisins

1 small bunch mint leaves

1 bunch chives —
   finely chopped

1 Combine all the vinaigrette ingredients in the bottom of a large salad bowl and whisk together vigorously.

2 Put the pine nuts, fennel, mustard and coriander seeds in a small skillet placed over medium heat. Toast them until the nuts turn a pale golden color and the spices release their fragrance. Add the mixture to the vinaigrette and combine, and then place salad servers over the vinaigrette.

3 Place the remaining salad ingredients on top of the servers, ensuring that the greens stay out of the vinaigrette (otherwise the mache will get soggy).

4 Toss the salad well just before serving. Distribute evenly between eight salad plates.

White Nectarine Carpaccio with a Microgreen Salad

Microgreens are tiny versions of various lettuces, herbs and greens that are harvested when they are very small — usually no more than an inch or so in height. They are packed with nutrients and have the distinct flavor of the more mature plant. First used in high-end restaurants, they are now more widely available for commercial use. They are also apparently easy to grow. This is going to be my next garden project.

I like using a mix of slightly spicy microgreens containing baby arugula. They complement the sweet nectarines. You can also use white peaches in this salad.

Serves 8 people

8 white nectarines

6 oz microgreens

3–4 sprigs lemon thyme leaves — finely chopped

1/2 bunch chives — finely chopped

1 large handful basil leaves (different varieties if possible)

1/3 cup extra virgin olive oil

1 1/2 tablespoons pear Champagne vinegar or other white wine vinegar

Zest of 1 lemon

Sea salt and black pepper

1 Thinly slice the nectarines into disks — when you get to the pit, cut carefully around it so that you can take it out without splitting the nectarine in two.

2 Place the slices onto salad plates so that they overlap slightly and cover the entire surface of each plate. Work from the outside of the plate toward the center. It should look like one or two concentric circles.

3 Combine the microgreens with the thyme and chives in a medium-sized bowl. Mound the microgreens in the middle of each plate on top of the nectarines. Insert the basil leaves between the nectarine slices.

4 Combine the olive oil, vinegar and lemon zest in a small bowl and whisk together to form an emulsion. Add a pinch of salt and some pepper. Drizzle a little of the vinaigrette over the nectarines and the microgreens on each plate. Serve immediately.

Peach, Melon and Prosciutto Salad

As a small child in Provence, I ate melons that were sweet, juicy, intensely floral and tasted of honey. We would pick them surreptitiously from the field neighboring our farmhouse. They would be served with prosciutto on rustic wooden plates. It was one of the hallmarks of summer. Whenever I come across one of these melons, I am transported back to that field and to the markets of Provence. Evidently, that sensation is hereditary. On one of the photo shoot days for *Salade*, whilst I was preparing this salad, my daughter came into the kitchen and tasted a piece of the melon. She took one bite and exclaimed, "This makes me feel like I'm in France!"

Serves 8 people

1 Tuscan melon (sometimes called Tuscan cantaloupe) — halved, seeded, peeled and cut into thin slices

4 yellow freestone peaches — halved, pitted and cut into thin slices

4 white freestone peaches — halved, pitted and cut into thin slices

16–20 slices prosciutto

1 large handful arugula

1 bunch chives — finely chopped

4 tablespoons olive oil — use a good, fruity oil

Sea salt and freshly ground black pepper

4 oz mozzarella, goat cheese or feta cheese (optional)

1 Arrange all the melon and peach slices on a large platter or on individual plates, alternating the fruit. Dot the surface with the prosciutto. Sprinkle the chives and arugula leaves over the top and drizzle with olive oil. Add a pinch of salt and some black pepper.

You can also serve this with fresh mozzarella, goat cheese or feta.

Arugula, Basil and Cilantro Salad with Pistachio Dukkah-Crusted Pluots

I have fallen in love with dukkah, if it's possible to fall in love with a mixture of spices, herbs and nuts! It transforms dishes, and judging by the reaction I have had when people tasted this salad, I think they fell in love, as well.

Dukkah is wonderfully versatile. Even if you're not making this salad, you can use it in an abundance of dishes; sprinkled on some hummus or yogurt with some toasted pita, over roasted vegetables, in soups, added to eggs... well, you get the idea. This is what I love about cooking, trying new dishes and experimenting with ingredients.

Serves 8 people

For the pistachio dukkah and pluots:

1 tablespoon olive oil

1 tablespoon lemon juice

1 1/2 tablespoons Herbes de Poisson (or a mix of fennel seeds, mustard seeds and coriander seeds)

4 oz pistachios — chopped

2 tablespoons sesame seeds

1 tablespoon finely chopped fresh oregano

1 lb assorted pluots — quartered and pitted

For the salad:

8 oz arugula

1 1/2 cups packed basil leaves

1 cup packed cilantro leaves

For the vinaigrette:

2 tablespoons olive oil

1 tablespoon pear Champagne vinegar or white wine vinegar

1 teaspoon fig balsamic vinegar or plain balsamic

Large pinch of salt

8–10 grinds of black pepper

1 Combine all the dukkah ingredients (except the pluots) in a small bowl and mix together well. Pour the mixture into a small skillet placed over medium-high heat and cook for 2–3 minutes, until the pistachios are fragrant. Remove from the heat and transfer the mixture to a medium-sized bowl. Add the pluots and toss well to combine.

2 In a large salad bowl whisk together all the vinaigrette ingredients to form an emulsion. Place salad servers over the vinaigrette. Place the salad ingredients on top of the utensils.

3 When ready to serve, toss the salad and divide among eight plates. Top the salad with pistachio dukkah-crusted pluots.

TOMATOES

Heirloom Tomato
Salad

—

Tomato, Avocado and
Buffalo Mozzarella
Salad

—

Yellow Tomato and
Purple Basil Salad

—

Roasted Chidori Kale
and Cherry Tomato
Salad

—

Madame Martin's
Garden Salad

—

Green Tomato and
Toasted Pepitas Salad

Heirloom Tomato Salad

One of the great pleasures of summer is the plethora of tomatoes that flood the farmers' markets. This salad is a celebration of those tomatoes.

Serves 8 to 10 people

8 large heirloom tomatoes (different varieties) — thinly sliced horizontally

8–10 small heirloom tomatoes or cherry tomatoes — thinly sliced horizontally

3 tablespoons olive oil

1 tablespoon white wine vinegar

Large pinch of coarse sea salt or flake salt such as Maldon or Murray River

6–8 grinds of black pepper

2 tablespoons chives — finely chopped

1 Lay all the tomato slices, slightly overlapping one another, on a large platter. Place the small slices on top of the larger ones and alternate the colors.

2 Combine the olive oil, vinegar, salt and pepper in a small bowl and whisk together. Drizzle the vinaigrette all over the tomatoes. Sprinkle the salad with the chives and serve.

Tomato, Avocado and Buffalo Mozzarella Salad

As the irrepressible Julia Child once said, "You don't have to cook fancy or complicated masterpieces — just good food from fresh ingredients." This is a simple salad, and the key to its success is excellent mozzarella, the fresher the better, avocados that are just ripe, and fat, juicy, flavorful tomatoes.

Arranging all the slices between one and the other may look a little elaborate, and, yes, may take a smidge more time, but I think it's worth the effort. If you're in a crashing hurry you can, of course, skip this, and just chop everything up into a bowl, it will still taste delicious!

Serves 8 people

For the salad:

6 oz assorted sprouts and microgreens

8 medium-sized heirloom tomatoes — thinly sliced

2 large ripe avocados — halved and pitted

2 balls fresh buffalo mozzarella — thinly sliced

1 packed cup thinly sliced mint leaves

2 tablespoons finely chopped chives

Pink flake salt

Black pepper

For the vinaigrette:

1/4 cup lemon olive oil

2 tablespoons lemon juice

1 Place the microgreen-sprout mixture across the bottom of a large shallow platter, or if plating individual portions, divided among eight soup bowls.

2 Place the sliced tomatoes in two parallel rows on top of the sprouts.

3 Using a small knife, carefully slice the avocado flesh into thin horizontal slices. I like to do this by cutting the avocado inside the skin, being careful not to pierce the skin, and then gently working a spoon between the flesh and the skin to scoop the slices out.

4 Intersperse the avocado slices with the tomatoes in one row of the tomato slices. Then, intersperse the tomatoes in the second row with the buffalo mozzarella slices.

5 Sprinkle the chopped mint and chives between the two rows of tomatoes.

6 In a small bowl, whisk together the olive oil and lemon juice to form an emulsion. Pour the vinaigrette over the tomatoes. Sprinkle the salad with a large pinch or two of flake salt and 4-5 grinds of black pepper.

Yellow Tomato and Purple Basil Salad

This salad came about because of the colorful sunflower yellow tomatoes, and the purple basil that was in a basket alongside, that I saw at a local farm stand. The colors were brilliant together, so I had to try mixing the two and, honestly, how can you go wrong with tomatoes and basil? This salad is easy to make, gorgeous to look at, fresh and bursting with flavor.

Serves 8 people

3 tablespoons olive oil

1 tablespoon white wine vinegar

Zest and juice of 1 lemon

1 1/2 lbs small and large yellow tomatoes — halved and the larger ones cut into wedges

1 small bunch purple basil leaves

Sea salt and freshly ground black pepper

1 Combine the olive oil, vinegar, lemon zest and juice in a large salad bowl. Whisk together to form a smooth emulsion. Place salad utensils over the vinaigrette.

2 Add all the tomatoes and basil on top of the utensils. When you are ready to serve the salad, toss it gently so that everything is well combined. Sprinkle some coarse sea salt or flake salt and some freshly ground pepper over the salad.

Roasted Chidori Kale and Cherry Tomato Salad

Last October, during the Eat Local Challenge (the full story of the challenge is in the introduction to this book), I made a new salad, sourced from local ingredients, every day. This was the salad I made at the midway point, day fourteen. A friend posted a comment on my Instagram feed saying, "You should spray these dishes and preserve them as works of art," to which I replied, "but they taste so good!" I hope you enjoy them as much as I enjoyed creating (and eating) them.

Serves 8 people

1 lb Chidori kale

Olive oil

Coarse sea salt

Black pepper

Juice of 1 lemon

1 lb cherry tomatoes

1/4 lb radish sprouts

1/4 lb ash covered goat cheese

1 tablespoon white wine vinegar or Champagne vinegar

1 Preheat the oven to 350 degrees.

2 Place the kale onto a baking sheet and drizzle with a little olive oil. Sprinkle with a large pinch of salt and 8-10 grinds of pepper. Cook for 8 minutes. Remove from the oven and pour the lemon juice over the kale. Once cooked, place the kale and any juice from the pan into a large salad bowl or shallow serving platter.

3 While the kale is roasting, prepare the tomatoes. Pour a little olive oil into a large skillet placed over medium heat. Add the cherry tomatoes, a good pinch of salt and 5–6 grinds of pepper. Cook for 8–10 minutes, shaking the pan once or twice. The tomatoes will become slightly wrinkled and will render some juice. Add the cooked tomatoes and any juice to the salad bowl.

4 Tuck small bundles of the sprouts into the kale-tomato salad, and then dot the salad with pieces of goat cheese.

5 Whisk together 2 tablespoons olive oil with the vinegar, and pour over the warm kale and tomatoes. Serve immediately.

Madame Martin's Garden Salad

This salad originally came about decades ago, at the end of a long hot summer in France where I had spent the better part of two months celebrating the end of high school. With me on this grand adventure was my long-time cohort, Anya, whom I had met on my first day of kindergarten, and remained firm friends with ever since.

At some point we realized that our dwindling funds might not quite stretch to the end of our planned stay, and in need of extra sustenance, we did a little local foraging. The foraging in question took place in the field next to the house, which was dripping in achingly beautiful tomatoes and bushels of basil. We had some canned corn in the house, so I made a vinaigrette and added the freshly harvested crop of tomatoes. We liked the salad so much, we repeated this for a few more days. One morning, I found Madame Martin standing between the rows of tomatoes. I should mention at this point that she was the formidable, octogenarian owner of said field, and therefore, everything that grew in it. I stood rooted to the ground, looking at her very much like Peter Rabbit, having been found out by Mr. McGregor. Luckily for me, she didn't try to run me through with a pitch fork, but rather smiled, nodded her head at her plants, and knowingly said, "they're good, aren't they!" I nodded, mortified, and apologized fifty times for having helped myself. She smiled again, held up her hand, and said, in her lilting Provencal accent, "all you had to do was ask."

I still love the salad, and think of her every time I make it, always remembering her generosity and the valuable lessons I learned that day. And no, in case you're wondering, I haven't foraged without permission since.

Serves 8 people

For the vinaigrette:

3 tablespoons olive oil

1 tablespoon white wine vinegar

1 teaspoon balsamic vinegar

Pinch of sea salt

6-8 grinds of black pepper

For the salad:

1 1/2 lbs assorted heirloom tomatoes — chopped

2 ears corn — shucked and kernels sliced off the cob

1/4 cup packed small basil leaves

1 In a large salad bowl, whisk together all the vinaigrette ingredients to form an emulsion. Place salad servers over the vinaigrette.

2 Add the chopped tomatoes, corn and basil leaves to the salad bowl. When ready to serve, toss gently to combine.

TOMATOES

Green Tomato and Toasted Pepitas Salad

I have tried, in vain, to grow these beautiful green tomatoes. I adore their color, texture and flavor, particularly the Green Zebra and Aunt Ruby varieties. Every year I plant some, convinced that I have finally mastered their cultivation, but alas, once again, they have eluded me. Fortunately, very talented, local farmers grow them with enviable ease, and I snap them up when I see them at the market. This salad shows off these tomatoes in all their glory with the sautéed pepitas adding a lovely delicate, nutty flavor to the dish.

Be sure to use green tomato varieties in this salad, not tomatoes which are green because they are not ripe.

Serves 8 people

6-8 green heirloom tomatoes — thinly sliced horizontally

1 tablespoon olive oil

1/3 cup raw pepitas (raw pumpkin seeds)

1 tablespoon finely chopped chives

Pinch of sea salt

5-6 grinds of black pepper

1 tablespoon basil olive oil

1 tablespoon balsamic vinegar (fig balsamic if possible)

1 Cover the center of a large shallow platter with the sliced tomatoes, slightly overlapping the slices.

2 Heat the olive oil in a small skillet placed over medium heat. Add the pepitas and sauté for 1-2 minutes until they just turn brown. Add the chives, salt and pepper, stir, and then cook for 30 seconds more. Remove from the heat and immediately spoon the hot pepitas mixture on top of the tomatoes.

3 In a small bowl, whisk together the basil olive oil and vinegar. Pour the vinaigrette over the tomatoes and serve.

ZUCCHINI & CORN

Grilled Corn Salad
with Pine Nut Pesto

—

Spinach and Zucchini
Ribbon Salad

—

Shaved Yellow
Squash, Corn and
Avocado Salad

—

Roasted Carrots,
Parsnips, Zucchini
and Onion Salad

—

Grilled Zucchini and
Tarragon Roasted
Chicken Salad

—

Stuffed Squash
Blossom Salad

Grilled Corn Salad with Pine Nut Pesto

I grew up in London, where, for the majority of the year, the weather could best be described as dismal and damp. Not weather conducive to barbecues. In fact, we didn't own one, so anything grilled took on a slightly exotic feel, and was something to look forward to.

The first time I ate grilled corn was at a picnic-cum-barbecue in my grandparents' garden in France. These were elaborate affairs. The women in the family prepared prodigious amounts of food. The men in the family all gave their opinions about the proper techniques to achieve the perfect *braise* (the moment when the charcoal is at its optimum) and how long each item should be cooked for. A playful banter ping-ponged back and forth between them, until finally everything was ready, shouts of *"à table"* echoed in the garden, and all the kids came scampering to devour the adults' hard work. The corn would be served with salted butter melting down its charred golden sides. This has always been the taste of summer for me, and this salad is a little tribute to those magical days.

Serves 8 people

For the salad:

3 ears fresh corn — shucked

Olive oil

Coarse salt

8 oz mixed salad greens

8 oz yellow carrots — peeled and thinly sliced

8 radishes — ends trimmed, then thinly sliced

1/4 cup cilantro leaves

For the pesto:

1/4 cup pine nuts

3 tablespoons finely chopped chives

1/4 cup olive oil

2 tablespoons lemon juice

1 teaspoon white wine vinegar

Large pinch of salt

8–10 grinds of black pepper

1 Pre-heat a grill pan over medium-high heat.

2 Place the corn on a plate and drizzle with a little olive oil, a good pinch of salt and 6–8 grinds of black pepper. Turn to coat well. Grill the corn cobs for approximately 1–2 minutes per side, turning them two or three times just until they start to color. Place the grilled corn on a cutting board, and when cool enough to handle, slice off the kernels.

3 Place the salad greens in a shallow salad bowl or large serving platter. Scatter the carrots, radishes, grilled corn kernels and cilantro leaves over the greens.

4 Place the pine nuts and chives in a food processor fitted with a metal blade. Pulse until they form a rough paste. Add the remaining pesto ingredients and process until well blended, but still a little coarse. Spoon the pesto over the salad and serve.

Spinach and Zucchini Ribbon Salad

This is a quick, light and easy salad to prepare. It looks elaborate, but the lovely zucchini curls are simply created by continuously peeling the zucchini. The salad also keeps very well, and for that reason I love to take this on picnics.

Serves 8 people

For the vinaigrette:

3 tablespoons olive oil

Zest and juice of 1 lemon

Zest and juice of 1 lime

Pinch of sea salt

For the salad:

4 zucchini

2 yellow squash

4 oz baby spinach leaves

$1/3$ cup pistachios

1 tablespoon finely chopped chives

Coarse sea salt

Black pepper

1 In a medium-sized salad bowl, whisk together the vinaigrette ingredients to form an emulsion. Place salad servers over the vinaigrette.

2 Trim the ends of the zucchini and the squash. Using a vegetable peeler, peel them entirely into long ribbons.

3 Place the zucchini and squash ribbons, spinach, pistachios and chives into the salad bowl. When ready to serve, toss to coat the salad well. Season with a good pinch of salt and 8–10 grinds of pepper.

Shaved Yellow Squash, Corn and Avocado Salad

Shaving zucchini and summer squash has become a favorite technique of mine this year. It makes salads look dramatic and beautiful. This is a lovely salad to prepare for a large gathering. I like to make it on a wide, flat platter, creating different patterns with the curls. It looks different each time, and that is part of the charm.

Serves 8 people

For the vinaigrette:

1 tablespoon walnut mustard or Dijon mustard

¼ cup olive oil

2 teaspoons white wine vinegar or Champagne vinegar

Sea salt

Black pepper

For the salad:

2 tablespoons finely chopped chives

¼ cup finely chopped basil leaves

8 ears of fresh corn — shucked and kernels cut off the cob

2 avocados — halved, pitted, flesh scooped out and cubed

4–6 yellow squash

1 In a medium-sized mixing bowl, whisk together the mustard, olive oil and vinegar to form a thick emulsion resembling a light mayonnaise. Season the vinaigrette with a good pinch of salt and 4–5 grinds of pepper. Place serving utensils over the vinaigrette.

2 Add the chives, basil leaves, corn kernels and cubed avocado to the mixing bowl, but do not toss just yet.

3 Trim the yellow squash ends and discard. Using a vegetable peeler, peel the squash entirely, lengthwise, creating long thin strips.

4 To assemble the salad, gently toss the ingredients in the mixing bowl, taking care not to crush the avocado cubes. Mound the mixture in the center of a large serving platter, or shallow bowl.

5 To create the squash curls, carefully roll up each squash strip, leaving a 2-inch "tab." Tuck the tab of the squash curls into the edge of the mounded corn salad to anchor the curls into place. Some of the curls will unwind themselves a little and that's part of the charm. Place the curls facing different directions so that some of the strips curl away from each other. Group 5–7 curls in clusters around the base of the salad. Season the salad with a little more salt and pepper.

Roasted Carrots, Parsnips, Zucchini and Onion Salad

This is a salad that can be eaten hot, cold or at room temperature. It's also great the next day. The salad tends to be a little different each time you make it — at least it is each time I make it. I use the ingredients I have in my fridge at the time, so there may be more zucchini in it or carrots or parsnips depending on the season and what I found at the market.

I'd love to say that all these vegetables come out of my garden, but my green thumb only seems to stretch as far as herbs and flowers, a few tomatoes and a little chard. My zucchini plants failed completely this year, and I was really looking forward to the patty pan squash I planted. Oh well, maybe next year.

Serves 8 to 10 people

For the vegetables:

3–4 patty pan squash — ends trimmed and then cut into wedges — try to use different varieties

2–3 green zucchini — ends trimmed, split lengthways and then sliced

4–5 carrots — peeled and sliced

4 small to medium parsnips — peeled, quartered and sliced

1 large red onion — peeled, halved and cut into thin slices

Juice of 2 lemons

5–6 sprigs of thyme

Olive oil

Sea salt and black pepper

For the herb pesto:

4 tablespoons fruity olive oil

Juice and zest of 2 lemons

1 large handful parsley — chopped

1 large handful cilantro — roughly chopped

1 large handful basil leaves

2 tablespoons chives — chopped

1 clove garlic

1 Preheat the oven to 375 degrees.

2 Place all the vegetables in a roasting pan and drizzle with olive oil. Squeeze the lemons over the vegetables and add the thyme, a dash or two of salt and 4–5 grinds of pepper. Roast the vegetables in the oven for 25–30 minutes. The carrots and zucchini can have a little crunch, but the parsnips do need to be cooked through, so check those in particular.

3 While the vegetables are roasting, prepare the herb pesto. Place all the pesto ingredients into a blender or food processor (liquids first — it makes it easier to process the pesto) and run it until you have a relatively smooth pesto. Check the seasoning. Depending on the size of the lemons you use, you may need a dash more. It should be bright green and very fresh tasting. Pour the pesto into a salad bowl and add the roasted vegetables to the bowl as soon as they are cooked. Toss while they are still warm.

Grilled Zucchini and Tarragon Roasted Chicken Salad

Poulet a l'estragon (tarragon chicken) was — actually still is — one of the dishes that I always looked forward to when visiting France. It's classic bistro fare, or *cuisine bourgeoise.* In other words, good home cooking.

Deft use of tarragon is key, as the slightly anise-flavored herb can be overpowering if used in large quantities. I always think of it as the quintessential French herb. It's used in a number of classic sauces, Béarnaise being the most well known.

This salad pairs moist tarragon roasted chicken with grilled zucchini and a mustardy vinaigrette.

Serves 8 people

3 ½ lbs whole chicken

2 yellow onions — peeled and thinly sliced

Olive oil

4 sprigs tarragon to roast with the chicken, plus the leaves from 1-2 more sprigs for the finished salad

Sea salt and black pepper

1 tablespoon Dijon mustard

4 tablespoons olive oil

1 tablespoon tarragon vinegar or white wine vinegar

5 zucchini — ends trimmed away and then sliced on a bias

1 Preheat the oven to 400 degrees.

2 Cover the bottom of a roasting pan with the sliced onions. Place the chicken on top and drizzle with a little olive oil. Tuck the tarragon sprigs around the chicken. Sprinkle a little salt and then grind some black pepper over the chicken. Roast for 90 minutes.

3 Spoon the mustard into the bottom of a large salad bowl. Pour in the olive oil and vinegar and whisk together well. It will look like mayonnaise. Place the serving utensils on top of the vinaigrette.

4 Pour a little olive oil into a large mixing bowl and add all the zucchini slices, a pinch of salt and some pepper. Toss to coat.

5 Place a grill pan on top of a stove and heat until it gets nice and hot. Grill the zucchini slices so that they are just cooked. Turn them after 2 minutes. You may have to do this in batches as all the slices may not fit on the grill in one layer. Add the grilled zucchini to the salad bowl.

6 Place the cooked chicken on a cutting board and let rest for 10 minutes before carving. Carve the chicken, removing all the meat and chopping it up into bite-sized pieces. Add the chicken pieces, the sliced roasted onions from the roasting pan, and the fresh tarragon leaves to the bowl.

7 When you are ready to serve, toss the ingredients well so that everything gets nicely coated with the vinaigrette.

Stuffed Squash Blossom Salad

I was invited to a Fourth of July barbecue this year and was contemplating what to bring as my contribution, when I spied squash blossoms at the market. Not the most traditional barbecue fare I know, but I couldn't resist!

The lovely thing about squash blossoms is that you can stuff them with so many things. I've added some left-over roast chicken to this recipe for a heartier version, and made another with roasted eggplant added to the mix. They are all delicious. Have fun experimenting!

Serves 8 people

Olive oil

1 red onion — peeled and finely diced

4 green onions — finely sliced

Salt

Black pepper

1/2 lb baby spinach

1/2 cup couscous

1/2 cup boiling water

8 oz whole milk ricotta

2 tablespoons finely chopped chives

2 tablespoons finely chopped parsley

1/4 cup lightly toasted pine nuts

2 tablespoons lemon olive oil

Zest and juice of 1 lemon

16 small zucchini with fresh squash blossoms attached

1 Preheat the oven to 400 degrees.

2 Pour a little olive oil into a large pan over medium-high heat. Add the red and green onions, a good pinch of salt and 10–12 grinds of pepper, and sauté until lightly golden brown, stirring frequently for 4–5 minutes.

3 Add the spinach to the onions and sauté an additional 1-2 minutes, until the spinach is just wilted. Transfer the onion and spinach mixture to a large mixing bowl.

4 Place the couscous into a small, heat-proof mixing bowl. Pour 1/2 cup boiling water and a pinch of salt over the couscous, stir to combine and cover for 10 minutes. Remove the lid and fluff the couscous with a fork, making sure to break up any clumps.

5 Add the cooked couscous, ricotta, chives, parsley, pine nuts, lemon olive oil and the lemon juice and zest to the spinach and onion mixture. Season with a generous pinch of salt and 10–12 grinds of pepper. Stir gently to combine.

6 Using a small spoon, carefully open, and then fill the squash blossoms with the spinach-couscous mixture. The blossoms are delicate, so take care not to tear them. Gently twist the top of each blossom to encapsulate the filling.

7 Place the stuffed squash blossoms onto a sheet pan or large shallow roasting dish. Drizzle with a little olive oil and turn to coat them. Roast in the oven for 15–20 minutes. The zucchini are ready when they are fork tender and the blossoms turn pale golden color. Serve immediately.

Suppliers & Sources

I am often asked where I buy my produce, fish, meat, flowers and wine. These purveyors, shops and markets are the ones I use whilst in California. They have all proven to be reliable, and I heartily recommend them.

SANTA BARBARA

CHEESE

C'est Cheese
www.cestcheese.com

The best local shop for exquisite cheeses and gourmet items, run by the charming Kathryn and Michael Graham.

HERBS AND SPICES

Pascale's Kitchen
www.pascaleskitchen.com

A great resource for exotic salts, herbs, spice blends and olive oils, and beautiful kitchen items.

PRODUCE

Santa Barbara's Farmers Market
One of the best markets on the West Coast.

www.sbfarmersmarket.org

At the market, I would highly recommend the following farms:

> **BD's Earthtrine Farms**
> Fragrant herbs and wonderful vegetables.
>
> **Fat Uncle Farms**
> They have THE most incredible blistered almonds.
>
> **Ojai Valley Sprouts**
> Source of the most beautiful microgreens.
>
> **Flying Disc Ranch**
> My favorite dates.
>
> **Roots Organic Farm**
> Spectacular salads and vegetables from Jacob Grant abound at this stand.
>
> **The Garden of .....**
> For the most beautiful and flavorful lettuce, herbs, leeks and carrots.

Mesa Produce
This store is an excellent source for locally-farmed organic produce.

SEAFOOD

Santa Barbara Fish Market
www.sbfish.com

Excellent local market at the harbor where you can buy fresh fish that have come right off the local boats.

LOS ALAMOS

BREAD

Bob's Well Bread
Fantastic naturally leavened breads and baked goods.

LOS ANGELES

BREAD

Republique
www.republiquela.com

Superb breads and pastries.

Gjusta
www.gjusta.com

Opened in 2014 to acclaimed reviews, this bakery/hip Venice deli produces extraordinary crunchy luscious bread.

CHEESE

The Cheese Store
www.cheesestorebh.com

The best cheese shop in Los Angeles, with more than 400 fabulous cheeses and other delicious culinary products.

GOURMET FOODS

Monsieur Marcel
www.mrmarcel.com

Wonderful array of gourmet foods and cheese from France with an incredible selection of mustards, oils and vinegars.

Eataly
www.eataly.com/us_en/stores/los-angeles

Massive Italian food emporium with a spectacular selection of pastas and rice, cured meats and cheese.

PRODUCE & FLOWERS

Santa Monica's Wednesday Farmers Market
www.santa-monica.org/farmers_market

This huge, diverse market supplies many of Los Angeles's great restaurants. It's worth a trip just to explore all sorts of seasonal goodies. One of my favorite vendors there is **Windrose Farms**.

SEAFOOD

Santa Monica Seafood
www.smseafoodmarket.com

A wonderful seafood store that supplies many of the top restaurants in Southern California. Their retail outlet is spectacular.

SAN FRANCISCO BAY AREA

BREAD

Tartine Bakery and Tartine Manufactory
www.tartinebakery.com

Yes, the line is worth the wait. The bread is that good.

PRODUCE & FLOWERS

The Ferry Plaza Farmers Market
Open on Tuesday, Thursday and Saturday. It is renowned throughout the country for both the quality and diversity of its fresh farm products, and artisan and prepared foods. One of my favorite places to visit in the Bay Area.

www.ferrybuildingmarketplace.com/farmers-market/

Berkeley Bowl
www.berkeleybowl.com

Iconic grocery store located in Berkeley, CA. It has a vast bulk food section and a extraordinary selection of fresh organic foods. Salad and mushroom heaven.

Index

Acknowledgments

This beautiful book came about with the help of a wonderful team of multi-talented and creative people.

I would like to thank all the extraordinary farmers whose produce appears on these pages: Jacob Grant from Roots Organic Farm, BD (Robert Dautch) from Earthtrine Farms, everyone at The Garden of....., Norma Ortiz from Ojai Valley Sprouts, Deb from Drake Family Farms, and everyone at Avila and Sons, Burkdoll Farms, Flying Disc Ranch, Her Family Farm and Regier Farm. I am in awe of your green thumbs. Every week, whatever the weather, you arrive at the farmers' market and pile your tables high with the fruits (and vegetables) of your labor. Your food is not only beautiful but soul satisfying. So much of the inspiration for my writing, cooking, and the recipes in this book comes from walking through the market and seeing the delicious food you have grown. You nourish my creativity. Thank you for your incredibly hard work in making our food landscape a more wholesome one.

To Harriet Whaley: Thank you for checking the sequencing of all the new recipes in this book. It is painstaking work, and I hugely appreciate the time and effort you took to make sure that all of these recipes flowed in the right order!

To Susan Noble: A massive thank you for all you do and for all your efforts on my behalf. You are the proofing queen! These books would not be here without you and the entire publishing team at M27 Editions.

To Ruth Verbois: Thank you for handling the myriad details of getting this, and all my books, out the door and into the hands of our booksellers and book buyers. You always handle so many details with aplomb. Thank you for helping make the first three books in this series — *Salade*, *Les Fruits* and *Les Legumes* — such a success; I look forward to our continued adventures with *Salade II*.

To the master photographer, and teacher Mike Verbois: Incredibly, this is our ninth book together! Thank you for teaching me so much about food photography. I could hear your words of wisdom as I shot the new images for this book. Your deft touch in processing all these files is apparent in the beautiful finished product! I am, as always, extraordinarily grateful for your energy, your patience, your fine eye and your art. *Merci* Mike!

To Judi Muller: This is our ninth cookbook together and every single page is beautiful. Thank you for your gorgeous and elegant graphic design. Most of all, thank you for your friendship, and making our collaboration such an enjoyable one. I look forward to new projects in the future.

To Shukri Farhad: What an extraordinary journey we have been on over the past 16 years, through the production, printing, publishing and promotion of all my cookbooks. Thank you for your unwavering belief in my work, and for championing my endeavors. Thank you, too, to Tracy for leading the cheering section and encouraging every road trip and promotional event we have taken. I could not do this without the limitless support of you both. Once again, *Merci!*

To Sherry Mannello: Words fail me entirely when it comes to you, Sherry. Your continuous help in the kitchen and behind the scenes, your enthusiasm, positive energy and unwavering devotion to this, and all my projects, is nothing short of stupendous. I am truly in awe and humbled by your efforts on my behalf over the past ten years. Thank you is just not enough!

The last year has seen huge upheavals, moving and relocations. I have been working on this book through all of these migrations. To my children, Olivia and Alexandre, once again you have endured the upheaval in the house, the time spent on this project and my endless recipe testing — although hopefully you enjoyed that part! I appreciate your patience with all my ventures and peregrinations, and treasure your words of encouragement throughout the production of *Salade II*. I adore you both more than you could ever know. *Merci mes enfants.*

To my parents: What an adventure our lives have been! You have opened up the world to me, and allowed me to dream. Your expectations, and belief in me, have driven me to new heights. I am so grateful that you always encouraged me, and assumed that these dreams were achievable, not letting flag when I had moments of doubt, but rather, always seeing that possibilities abound. My books would not be here without you. Thank you is not enough for your unflagging support. *Encore, encore, mille fois merci.*